THE ANGUISH OF THOUGHT

A UNIVOCAL BOOK
Drew Burk, Consulting Editor
Univocal Publishing was founded by Jason Wagner and Drew Burk as an independent publishing house specializing in artisanal editions and translations of texts spanning the areas of cultural theory, media archeology, continental philosophy, aesthetics, anthropology, and more. In May 2017, Univocal ceased operations as an independent publishing house and became a series with its publishing partner the University of Minnesota Press.

Univocal authors include:

Miguel Abensour
Judith Balso
Jean Baudrillard
Philippe Beck
Simon Critchley
Fernand Deligny
Jacques Derrida
Vinciane Despret
Georges Didi-Huberman
Jean Epstein
Vilém Flusser
Barbara Glowczewski
Évelyne Grossman
Félix Guattari
David Lapoujade
François Laruelle

David Link
Sylvère Lotringer
Jean Malaurie
Michael Marder
Quentin Meillassoux
Friedrich Nietzsche
Peter Pál Pelbart
Jacques Rancière
Lionel Ruffel
Michel Serres
Gilbert Simondon
Étienne Souriau
Isabelle Stengers
Eugene Thacker
Siegfried Zielinski

THE ANGUISH OF THOUGHT

Évelyne Grossman

Translated by Matthew Cripsey
and Louise Burchill

A UNIVOCAL BOOK

University of Minnesota Press
Minneapolis | London

The University of Minnesota Press acknowledges the contribution of Jason Wagner, Univocal's publisher, in making this volume possible.

Originally published in French as *L'Angoisse de penser.* Copyright 2008 by Les Éditions de Minuit, 7, rue Bernard-Palissy, 75006 Paris.

Published by the University of Minnesota Press
111 Third Avenue South, Suite 290
Minneapolis, MN 55401–2520
http://www.upress.umn.edu

ISBN 978-1-5179-0670-2 (pb)
A Cataloging-in-Publication record for this book is available from the Library of Congress.

Printed in the United States of America on acid-free paper

The University of Minnesota is an equal-opportunity educator and employer.

25 24 23 22 21 20 19 18   10 9 8 7 6 5 4 3 2 1

Works of art are always the products of having been at risk, of having pursued an experience to the very end, to the utmost limit of human endeavor.

—Letter from Rilke to Clara

CONTENTS

Translators' Prefatory Note | *ix*

Acknowledgments | *xv*

Out of Oneself | *1*

The Voices of Jacques Derrida | *33*

Emmanuel Levinas's Seed of Folly | *55*

"There Is No Such Thing as Metalanguage":
    Lacan and Beckett | *71*

What Is an Archive? Beckett, Foucault | *87*

At the Limit . . . : A Reading of Samuel Beckett's
    That Time | *107*

Blanchot Hero | *127*

Blanchot's Anagrams: A Reading of *Thomas
    the Obscure* | *139*

Bibliographical Note | *157*

Notes | *159*

TRANSLATORS' PREFATORY NOTE

L'Angoisse de penser—the title of this book in French and, accordingly, the "experience" Évelyne Grossman elucidates at the heart of the writing by twentieth-century authors having accepted the risk of madness in thought—immediately introduces the major problem, or nexus of decision, confronted in this text's translation. Given that *angoisse* can be rendered as either "anguish" or "anxiety" and that each of these terms has acquired a signature status in works available to English-language readers by one or more of the writers and philosophers Grossman considers, on what grounds are we to decide which of these English "equivalents" best conveys the "seemingly destructive and dehumanizing experience" alongside which thought would emerge? Is it, in sum, a matter of the *anguish* of thought or, rather, of the *anxiety*?

The opening chapter to Grossman's book, consisting as it does precisely in an exposition of the *angoisse* confronted, explored, and finally surmounted by the authors she focuses on, provides a number of key considerations for the adjudication of this "point" of translation. The first of these is the distinction Grossman draws between the "literary, metaphysical" *angoisse* that is the object of her inquiry and the more "humdrum" *anxiété* that afflicts not only those who seek recourse for this "symptom" in doctors' offices and over-the-counter prescriptions but, all in all, a fair percentage of the population of our contemporary Western societies on a more-or-less daily basis. Now, this distinction well seems to militate for reserving "anguish" for the "metaphysical" affect/experience that furnishes, on Grossman's analysis, the "obligatory gateway into writing," while employing "anxiety"—in conformity with both specialized and everyday English—for the widespread malaise that cedes to anxiolytics and other antidepressants. Etymologically, moreover—although this is a point we will need to return to—"anguish" is directly related to *angoisse* just as "anxiety" is to *anxiété.* On closer inspection, however, things are not quite so clear-cut, for while "anxiety" does indeed designate in English the medical and psychological trouble Grossman refers to here—as notably instanced in the recent invention of "Generalized Anxiety Disorder"— the same term also qualifies as the standard English "equivalent" of *angoisse* in its "metaphysical," speculative occurrences. It is, accordingly, as *The Concept of Anxiety* that Søren Kierkegaard's text *Begrebet Angest*—translated into French as *Le concept de l'angoisse*—has been rendered in English, with this text being precisely quoted by Grossman when she counterposes the "metaphysical heights" of *angoisse* to the more commonplace medicalizable *anxiété.* In addition to Kierkegaard, moreover, Grossman's first chapter references Heidegger, as well as—in veering away from the existentialist tradition to psychoanalysis—Freud and Lacan, all of whom proffer what is again, in English translation, an analytic/analysis of *anxiety.*[1] Clearly then, the latter term has been judged, by those tasked with the translation of these authors' texts, as "the best possible equivalent" of *angst, Angst,* and *angoisse.* Would the English language and the history of its philosophical/metapsychological translations oblige us, as such, to deploy / make do with "anxiety" in this dual acceptation: the cruel experience of thinking and writing, on the one hand, and the generalized trouble of worry and stress, on the other?

It is instructive at this juncture to return to considerations of etymology—and all the more so in that Évelyne Grossman herself, in a second key indication of the meaning she attributes to "literary, metaphysical" *angoisse*, underlines the French word's derivation from the Latin *angustia*, "narrowness," itself formed on *angustus*, "narrow." Both these Latin words hail from *ang(u)ere*—"to throttle or choke, to torment, to make narrow," with the root *ang* (or Proto-Indo-European **angh-*) found equally at the basis of the German *eng* (to which *Angst* is related) as well as a wide spectrum of English words having the sense of compression or tightness, among which, in addition to "anguish," notably figure "angina," "anger" . . . and "anxiety." That said, "anguish," which made its appearance in the English language circa 1200, is more directly related to *angoisse* than is "anxiety," being a strict cognate of the modern French term insofar as both are formed on the Old French *anguisse* or *angoisse*, and thereby on the Latin *angustia*. "Anxiety" dates, for its part, from the sixteenth century and, according to one etymological source,[2] was probably taken from the French *anxiété* although the adjective "anxious" must have been formed directly (as is the case, indirectly, for *anxiété*) on the Latin *anxius*, which is where we find again the root *ang(u)ere*—and, with this, the (indirect) kinship to *angoisse*. Interestingly, both "anxiety" and *anxiété* had predominantly a medical sense until the nineteenth century, when they then additionally acquired what English and French dictionaries characterize as a more "intellectual" or "spiritual" value. For James Strachey, the translator of Freud, "this well-established psychiatric, or at least medical, use" explains no doubt why "anxiety" came to be the word "universally, and perhaps unfortunately, adopted" in English for the translation of *Angst*—with Strachey stipulating the misfortune of this translation choice to lie in "anxiety"'s "current everyday meaning" (the "democratized" and "banalized" sense Grossman refers to), which renders it inadequate for the uses of *Angst*.[3] It is undoubtedly equally because of its established medical, or proto-psychiatric, use that "anxiety" is the commonly accepted translation of *angoisse* in not only its psychiatric or psycho-analytical occurrences but also its "metaphysical" ones—especially insofar as the latter would seem largely to stem, in the French philosophical tradition, from the concept introduced by Kierkegaard and set out, therefore, in what the latter described as a "psychological" exposition of hereditary sin.[4]

Given this determining influence of Kierkegaard's *Begrebet Angest* on the philosophical signification (and destiny) of *angoisse* in French texts from the late 1800s on, it is pertinent to note, in parallel, that, although *The Concept of Anxiety* is now the standard rendering of Kierkegaard's text in English, it first appeared in translation as *The Concept of Dread*. The translator who chose this title, Walter Lowrie, stipulates nonetheless that, while "dread" indicates "the distress of the moment," it fails to suggest what is essential to the experience Kierkegaard deals with: namely, "an apprehension of the future, a presentiment of a something which is 'nothing.'"[5] Retranslated some thirty-six years later (in 1980) as *The Concept of Anxiety,* Kierkegaard's book was to retain this title when once again presented in a new translation by Alastair Hannay in 2014. The reason for retaining "Anxiety" rather than "Dread," Hannay states, is not only because of this title's having now become standard but also for both etymological considerations and—in confirmation of the influence of the established medical use of "anxiety"—"the link, or contrast, [it forges] with psychiatric disorders with the same name (or 'Angst')."[6] In recalling Strachey's remark on the inadequacy of "anxiety" as a rendering for *Angst,* we might well wonder whether, were a link to the psychiatric use of "anxiety" not judged necessary, a more preferable choice of translation—and one with greater "metaphysical" resonance—would not have been "anguish." Does it not, after all, as Strachey goes on to note, describe a "still more acute condition" than that of anxiety, all while being equally related etymologically to *Angst* . . . just as it is (and still more closely so than "anxiety," as Strachey himself underlines) to *angoisse*?

The experience of *angoisse* Grossman's first chapter describes is one of "being out of oneself, an ecstatic or terrifying encounter with the Other, [and] an exercise in disidentification" that is crucially fueled, and harnessed, by the tireless energy of the negative (such as Blanchot, for example, was to situate "in the infinite heart of the passion of thought"). For Artaud, it is "a kind of suction cup placed on the soul"; for Bataille, a "chance," whatever the price to pay for it, for those who would create. That the *angoisse* of which these last two authors wrote has been rendered in the English translations of their work as "anguish" confirms—we would suggest—what considerations of etymological proximity, on the one hand, and the distance from both everyday and medicalizable "anxiety," on the other, have already inferred: "anguish" is the word in the English language that best conveys the experience— or "acute condition"—of ecstatic depersonalization that is linked to the capacity to think or write. *Angoisse* has accordingly been systematically rendered throughout this translation as "anguish," with the exception of occurrences in which "anxiety" imposes itself as obligatory. These latter consist predominantly of psychoanalytic or psychiatric references (e.g., Lacan, Freud, Janet, Ehrenberg); other— metaphysical or literary—references where "anxiety" is the established translation; and instances drawing on the "current everyday meaning" of "anxiety"/"anxiousness."

Wherever "anxiety" in this translation renders *anxiété,* rather than *angoisse,* this is signaled in the text.

L'Angoisse de penser—The Anguish of Thought . . . Our translation of this book has been guided by not only a concern of rigorous fidelity but equally by the desire that it do justice to the declaration on which Évelyne Grossman concludes her opening chapter: that reading is a joy!

ACKNOWLEDGMENTS

The translation of a work such as this requires, from all parties, a great deal of commitment and time, and often more of the latter than expected. With that in mind, we would like to extend our most sincere thanks to our editor, Drew Burk, for his infinite patience, however sorely we may have tested it. Moreover, his pertinent suggestions and invaluable guidance have been critical to the success of our project. We would also like to express our gratitude to the imprint's publisher, Jason Wagner, not only for his administrative support but also for his helpful remarks and truly anguishing cover design. Thanks, too, go to the other members of the team at Univocal and the University of Minnesota Press, whose combined support has been most gratefully received throughout the process. Then, of course, there is the author herself, Évelyne Grossman, whose meticulous reading of our text has been of the utmost help. This final translation owes much to her judicious remarks and generous attention.

OUT OF ONESELF

*. . . thought, at the level of its existence, in its very
dawning, is in itself an action—a perilous act.*
—Michel Foucault, *The Order of Things*

Anguish

Who has not experienced at least once that irksome feeling
of indeterminate disquiet that silently swells and prolifer-
ates, radiates and returns in waves: a knot in the pit of your
stomach, your throat constricted, making it impossible to
breathe, palpitations, a tightening around the ribcage or
the painful cramping of muscles? In his early writing, Antonin Artaud transfigures the symptom: "an anguish that
comes in flashes, that is punctuated by abysses as dense
and serried as insects, like a kind of tough vermin whose
every motion is arrested, an anguish in which the mind
strangles and cuts itself off—kills itself."[1] He was to add a
little later on: "One must have known this suction-like rise
of anguish whose waves cover you and fill you to bursting
as if driven by some intolerable bellows. An anguish that
approaches and withdraws, each time more vast, each time
heavier and more swollen. [. . .] It is a kind of suction cup
placed on the soul . . ."[2]

Something vile keeps trying to force its way in. One feels
an uncertain foreboding, an ill-defined threat. So the entire
body contracts as though it were hastily trying to seal off

1

the exits, batten down the hatches. Some, when struck by anxiety, curl into a ball, close themselves off; petrified, they wait for the attack to subside. The next stage of severity is a full-blown anxiety episode, panicked fear, the *emotional ictus* of which psychiatrists speak. Mostly, however, nothing of the sort occurs: our anxiety is an easygoing one.

The nausea that Jean-Paul Sartre describes is another form of the same disquiet, an unnerving sensation, like a hole opening up within. It is a tear through which I escape myself and stream out: a hemorrhage of being. I *seep* and flow outside, while the outside threatens to surge in, to engulf me, in the backwash. It is a nauseous ebb and flow that exposes the shortcomings of our corporeal and psychic envelopes. In anguish, being returns to a porous state, is disarmed—it is a hideous, infantine distress.

At the heart of modern writing, *anguish* designates that which occurs in closest proximity to thought. It is the narrow gate (*angustia*)[3] through which one must continually pass, barred by powerlessness [*impuissance*] and disgust; it is the price to be paid, the pound of flesh, for the spark of an idea—what we still call, and by no coincidence, "inspiration." Anguish is the obligatory gateway into writing: it is the *impower* [*impouvoir*] of which Artaud spoke, and later Maurice Blanchot and Jacques Derrida; for Samuel Beckett and Michel Foucault, it is the dizzying prospect of "how to begin"; for Jacques Lacan, the "abject experience" into which analytical writing delves; it is Georges Bataille's "I feel rotten"; and Emmanuel Levinas's shapeless swarming of being. All experience it differently, and yet there is a profound commonality to all these experiences in that they all rattle the assured bases of what we believe to be our own thought, our own identity. Thought is a trait of anguish. Martin Heidegger asked, "What is That which calls on us to think?"[4] Here, the question is rather, "How does thought emerge in such close proximity to the seemingly destructive and dehumanizing experience of anguish?" How can a nauseous anguish, that *yawning gap* to which Bataille alludes in *Inner Experience,* lead to inspiration (the voice of the Other in me; the "spirited-away" speech [*parole soufflée*] that Derrida heard in Artaud's work) and thereby transform the speaker or author so that he or she *is no longer merely him- or herself* (one person thinking and writing)? Writing is, then, this profound experience of de-personalization undertaken by the writers and thinkers of the twentieth century.

Is this literary, metaphysical anguish still our own? Is it indeed the same symptom designated today by such terms as *anxiety* [*anxiété*] and *stress,* which ultimately define that which responds to, or rather cedes to, anxiolytics and other antidepressants? Does it galvanize the sufferer to write, this banalized, democratized anxiety [*anxiété*] that fanciful be-havioral psychologists—following the invention of OCD (the famous obsessive-compulsive disorder)—have labeled "GAD" (generalized anxiety disorder)?[5] Most likely not. "Not just anyone can go mad," Lacan often said; to which Bataille adds: "Not just anyone can become anguished." To *think oneself into anguish* requires a patient asceticism, an experience that Bataille readily compares to the *Spiritual Exercises* of Ignatius of Loyola, founder of the Society of Jesus and one of the inspirations behind James Joyce's *Portrait of the Artist as a Young Man.* Bataille elucidates this point in *Inner Experience*:

> Anguish, obviously, is not learned. One would provoke it? It is possible: I hardly believe so. One can stir up the dregs of it . . . If someone admits of having anguish, it is necessary to show the inexistence of his reasons. He imagines the way out for his torments: if he had more money, a woman, another life . . . The foolishness of his anguish is infinite. Instead of going to the depths of his

anguish, the anxious one pratters, degrades himself and flees. Anguish however was his chance: he was *chosen* in accordance with his *forebodings.* But what a waste if he escapes: he suffers as much and humiliates himself, he becomes stupid, false, superficial. Anguish, once evaded, makes of a man an agitated Jesuit, but agitated to emptiness.[6]

The "agitated Jesuit"—is this the ultimate fate of today's humdrum anxiety sufferers, who fail to raise themselves to the metaphysical heights of anguish, and to whom the true apprenticeship of anguish in Søren Kierkegaard's sense of "supreme knowledge" and "drowning in possibility" remains lamentably unknown? Some would object to this as misplaced elitism. And rightly so. The anguish in question here does not possess the familiarity of our intimate fears, however violent they may be; it is the cruel *experience* of thinking and writing that does not belong to any therapeutics or *materia medica.* Blanchot called it the *demand* of writing. Nothing, then—unless the source runs dry—can cure what has come to be defined as being out of oneself, an ecstatic or terrifying encounter with the Other, an exercise in disidentification.[7]

Fatigue

Some fifteen years ago, in his deftly titled *The Weariness of the Self,* Alain Ehrenberg proposed an analysis of new forms of depression in contemporary Western societies. He highlighted the importance of the fact that the division between permission and interdiction, which until the 1950s–60s constituted the social norm for the integration of individuals, is today no longer effective. Slowly but surely, another division has established itself, one that separates the possible from the impossible; nowadays, Ehrenberg notes, while nothing is truly prohibited, neither is anything truly possible: "being ourselves makes us depressed. The anxiety of being oneself hides behind the weariness of the self."[8] Behind the lassitude of living, it is, then, once again anxiety that we find lurking.

At the turn of the last century, as Ehrenberg reminds us, there were two opposing theories of anxiety and depression: those of Freud and of Janet. For Freud, the depressive is someone ignorant of his or her guilt; the anxiety that grips him or her is the result of an unconscious guilt pertaining to the interdictions established by the superego. Insofar as neurosis is conceived in terms of conflict between desire and prohibition by Freud, *being oneself* requires a lengthy process of liberation from the unconscious taboos and proscriptions that paralyze the subject's freedom. In this sense, Ehrenberg suggests, the emancipation of the individual from his or her neurosis is the fruit of a struggle comparable to those fights for freedom undertaken by workers, women, and the colonized. The French psychiatrist Pierre Janet, contemporary and great rival of Freud, thought differently: for him, anxiety is a pathological inadequacy, a deficiency of energy. His theory of psychoasthenia in particular is largely based on the notion of a "reduction of psychological tension." His conception of anxiety centers not on conflict but on fatigue, asthenia, the unpleasant sensation of exhaustion, emptiness, and the inability to act.[9] Nowadays, confronted less with interdiction than with a cult of performance and efficiency ("to make a success of one's life"), the modern individual would seemingly suffer less from guilt than from "depressive breakdown." Ehrenberg declared this a posthumous victory for Janet over Freud.

Is the goal of analysis, in the Freudian sense of the term, truly to help the analysand reach that purportedly sovereign state of wellbeing: *to be oneself*? One might very much doubt it. This is why, and it is a point to which I shall return,

Lacan proposes an approach to the concept of anxiety that calls into question such simple definitions of the notion of "self." Nevertheless, the link between anxiety and fatigue, recalled by Ehrenberg, resonates in those voices as weary as they are tenacious, even sometimes heroic; those that, from Beckett to Barthes to Blanchot, reinvented the writing of depression. In the face of anguish, said Bataille, "A singular courage is necessary in order not to succumb to depression and to continue."[10]

Such courage is demonstrated both by Beckett's indefatigable "fatigued" one, the *exhausted* beyond all tiredness[11] who laboriously gets up and moves forward again, dragging his or her feet *tirelessly . . .* and also by the asthenic Belacqua, pitiable and humorous, balled up in an "old fetus" position, a familiar character in many of Beckett's texts, from *Murphy* to *Company*: both of whom are hilarious symbols of our contemporary anxieties.

The fatigued being that Levinas describes is not so different from Belacqua. Fatigue, he writes, is "a stiffening, a numbness, a way of curling up into oneself." Just like Beckett's beggar, Levinas's fatigued drags its feet: it can no longer keep up the pace, as though it is *lagging behind* its own existence. "Out of joint with itself, in a dislocation of the *I* from itself," it has become incapable of *joining up* with itself in the instant "in which it is nonetheless committed for good."[12] What, then, does the experience of fatigue, this "reverse inspiration" (fatigue being, in this sense, the inverse of ecstasy), reveal to us? That existence is an act, a "task to take up." Nowhere more so than in fatigue (or in laziness, its accomplice in sluggishness or, as psychiatrists call it, "psychomotor retardation") is existence so visibly ensnared in the process of stagnation that relentlessly threatens it, a movement that is "caught up in itself, showing that the verb 'to be' is a reflexive verb: one is not; rather one *is oneself* [*on n'est pas, on s'est*]":

There exists a weariness which is a weariness of everything and everyone, and above all *a weariness of oneself.*
What wearies then is not a particular form of our life—
our surroundings, because they are dull and ordinary,
our circle of friends, because they are vulgar and cruel;
the weariness concerns existence itself. Instead of
forgetting itself in the essential levity of a smile, where
existence is effected innocently, where it floats in its
fullness as though weightless and where, gratuitous and
graceful, its expansion is like a vanishing, in weariness
existence is like the reminder of a commitment to exist,
with all the seriousness and harshness of an irrevocable
contract. One has to do something, one has to aspire
after and undertake. In spite of the false smile of the
complete skeptic who, having suspended his judgments,
abstains from acting and from aspiring to anything, the
obligation of this contract remains incumbent on us like
an inevitable "one must."[13]

But more anguishing still—even if Levinas sometimes rejects
the term[14]—that which is brutally revealed in the depths of
fatigue, in those nights of insomnia that he describes so
arrestingly, is the anonymous "rustling of being," that pre-
ontological, prehuman murmur he names the *there is.* This
is what oozes from the walls and creeps in the darkness, like
a silent threat watching over "the insomnia of being." "The
rustling of the *there is* . . . is horror," writes Levinas, finding in the intensity of this terror echoes of Sartre's narrator upon discovering, before the roots of the chestnut tree,
existence as "the very paste of things."[15] For Levinas, too,
the *there is* is that being that is the being of no one, which
precedes the coming of any subject—a relentless current of
impersonal existence in which I usually bathe unknowingly.
Nausea appears again in a text of 1935 that Levinas was to
publish many years later, and in which he describes in detail

"the state of nausea that precedes vomiting, and from which vomiting will deliver us": "There is in nausea a refusal to remain there, an effort to get out. Yet this effort is always already characterized as desperate: in any case, it is so for any attempt to act or to think. And this despair, *this fact of being riveted, constitutes all the anxiety of nausea.* In nausea—which amounts to an impossibility of being what one is—we are at the same time riveted to ourselves, enclosed in a tight circle that smothers. We are there, and there is nothing more to be done [. . .]. However, this 'nothing-more-to-be-done' is the mark of a limit-situation in which the uselessness of any action is precisely the sign of the supreme instant from which we can only depart."[16]

Just as in the experience of the *there is,* Levinas discerns in nausea an untenable position: "twisted over itself in its skin, too tight in its skin, in itself already outside of itself," as he puts it in *Otherwise than Being.* Here, the revulsed body in its entirety attempts to purge itself, to tear itself from itself ("nausea sticks to us"), to turn itself inside out to escape, pass whole to the outside: nausea is this antagonism in which I am at the same time both bound and revolted from the inside ("our depths smother beneath ourselves"). At the heart of the anguish of the *there is* lies this contradictory trait of an impossible uprooting. Extracting oneself from the *there is*—declaring oneself existent—the subject acknowledges by the same gesture that he or she is *riveted to existence,* with shame and disgust succeeding anguish. Only much later did Levinas develop the most radical logic of this experience, that of a vertiginous asceticism, a relinquishment of myself that tears me from myself and carries me toward others—a response to the call of the other made by the *otherwise than being.*

I shall return later to Levinas's deliberately senseless

approach, but I wanted to highlight here the astonishing double anguish or fundamental *double bind* that first seizes his thought, itself fluctuating entirely between contraction and rupture: anguish over the limitation of being and anguish over the infiniteness of the prehuman. It is an unbearable ebb and flow from which one can only extricate oneself through a burst of strength that verges on a stroke of madness (or genius)—through the *beyond essence,* this "exposedness" of the self that he goes on to describe as "tearing-from-oneself-for-another."[17]

Doubtless nowhere more so than in Levinas's writing is being out of oneself—*ecstasy* in the etymological sense—revealed as straying on the fringes of madness, but also as that which most obstinately, and knowingly, explores it. Commenting on Aristotle's *Problem XXX* and its famous question, "Why is it that all men who have become outstanding are melancholic?" Jackie Pigeaud points out that he chose to render both the terms *ekstasis* and *mania* as *folie* [madness] when translating the work into French. "I am fully aware," he states, "that *ek-stasis* has readily been glossed as 'being out of oneself,' but it is indeed madness to which Aristotle refers when, following Galen, he defines melancholy as ecstasy, a disturbance in thought: 'Black bile, when overheated, seeks to escape. It can do this as a confusion of thought. It brings the individual out of himself.'"[18] "Ecstasy" is the term used in *Problem XXX* to portray the relationship between madness, the violence of melancholy, and the capacity to create. That thought—the anguish of thought—prowls the borders of madness, in a violent or blissful exit from oneself, was known by the writer-thinkers of the twentieth century better than anyone.

Ecstasy

On more than one occasion while writing *Inner Experience,* Georges Bataille consulted Pierre Janet's *From Anxiety to*

Ecstasy: Studies on Beliefs and Feelings [*De l'angoisse à l'extase. Etudes sur les croyances et les sentiments*], a work we know he borrowed several times from the French National Library in 1935 and 1942. Alongside other case studies in the publication, Janet recounts in detail the religious delirium of one of his patients, Madeleine, who was in his care for twenty-two years before returning home at the end of her life on account of a "relative recovery." In his notes to *Inner Experience,* Bataille quite harshly criticizes Janet's attitude toward his "ecstatic," accusing the psychiatrist, among other things, of a "paternal, ironic and, in a word, infinitely contemptuous benevolence."[19] There is little doubt that, in certain respects, Bataille felt closer to Madeleine than to her psychiatrist: it was a time at which he was seeking ways to explore the torments of ecstasy himself, which he saw as the only way to oppose what he so aptly called a "turning in on oneself," and enter into communication with "an elusive beyond." It suffices, that said, to read Janet's work to realize that Bataille's judgment was largely unfair. Indeed, what is on the contrary most striking is the open-mindedness, patience, and caring interest Janet demonstrated toward the woman he called Madeleine. He stresses not only how much he "esteems this woman's intelligence and moral sensitivity" but also "her genuine literary qualities."[20] The some two thousand pages of the journal Madeleine kept for him—a journal she began upon her hospitalization and in which she recorded how she felt and the details of her inner life—constitute the very core of Janet's work: he includes some very long passages to support his own observations, as well as several of the drawings she did. An extraordinarily rich document, Janet's book dialogues moreover with numerous psychiatric, philosophical, and religious works concerning the great Christian mystics, of which Madeleine is far from being just a pale, modern imitation.

Madeleine's moments of "ecstatic bliss," her excesses of sexual energy, are accordingly not so very different from the ineffable suffering and "burning passions" recounted by Madame Guyon and Teresa of Avila in their time. As Janet explains, Madeleine's ecstasy is filled with scenes of the Passion: she comes to the aid of Jesus in the Garden of Gethsemane; sometimes she herself is Jesus; she feels the thorns pierce her forehead; she is crucified and spends the entire night with her arms in the shape of the cross. On occasion, she even displayed small stigmata, which Janet photographed conscientiously while searching to provide a rational explanation. "There are great ecstatics and mediocre ecstatics," he notes with humor: "talent and practice play their part." What most interested Janet in his capacity as inventor of psychoasthenia, though, was the way Madeleine would alternate, like Kraepelin's manic depressives, between attacks of anxiety and attacks of ecstasy. During extreme bouts of anxious delirium, she would go through what she called terrible "states of torment," during which "the excess of evil" would give way to bizarre episodes of beatitude: "It seems," she writes, "that the more I suffer, the more I live and the happier I am; the measure of my suffering appears equal to the measure of bliss that God grants me." The intensity of a martyr's torment, Janet then notes, has often been remarked to determine that of his or her ecstatic joy. "There is, here, an inversion of emotions, the mechanism of which is little understood," he concludes, without any further explanation.

One cannot help but think here of the ecstatic smile of the Chinese torture victim whose image—captured in a series of photographs—haunted Bataille. "In the end, the patient writhed, his chest flayed, arms and legs cut off at the elbows and at the knees. His hair standing on end, hideous, haggard, striped with blood, beautiful as a wasp."[21] And Bataille recounts in *Inner Experience* how he used these distressing images in his attempts at "loss of self," with "the young and seductive Chinese man" communicating to him "the excessive nature of his pain." This brings us to the puzzling question of the secret bond between mysticism and torment, which Michel de Certeau has studied at length and in which the "stigmatized self" of a rejected subject, in its status as "waste," sees itself as *rot* and turns toward an outside, a *Beyond* of what it is and which exceeds it. The Christian mysticism of the sixteenth and seventeenth centuries is full of these fluctuations between the exaltation of degradation and forms of *hubris* (excess)—all of which constitute exits from oneself (the mystic is "outside of him- or herself"). Far from interpreting this as a pure manifestation of perverted masochism, Certeau emphasizes instead the complexity of the relationship between contempt (you are nothing but rot) and faith (there is something other).[22] Mysticism is, then, a melancholic passion that transfigures the religious scene into an amorous one, with faith becoming an "erotics of the Body-God"—the ever-recommenced celebration of the ecstatic wrenching away (pain and orgasm combined) from this object lost forever: the body of Christ gone from the tomb. Psychoanalysts would call this the eroticization of anxiety, and they are no doubt right; but what do we really know about this *passion of negativity* that, in anguish, transforms the coming of absence into joy, happiness . . . even writing?

Passion of Negativity

In an article paying homage to Georges Bataille published a few months after his death,[23] Blanchot highlighted the following, which is an essential point, I believe, to understanding the anguish of thinking and writing that this book considers: inner experience is, for Bataille, "a passion of negative thinking." How are we to interpret what Blanchot is saying here, and which clearly applies in his own case as well? I would suggest that, firstly, we take it to mean an indefatigable exploration of the *excess* of negativity. *Excess, overflow, impossible*: these are familiar words for readers of Bataille and designate that which is always escaping: this "surplus of 'negativity'" that attempts to push back the very limits of thought; the desubjectifying violence to which anyone who explores the destructive force of an endless and irreconcilable rejection is confronted. In this sense, inner experience is indeed the "limit-experience" Blanchot describes.

The essential logic of this experience, he suggests, might be grasped by comparing it to those two configurations it seems very similar to (yet must not be confused with): religious mysticism and the Hegelian dialectic. Blanchot accordingly queries whether the ecstatic rapture that Bataille explores should be attributed to a religious heritage of which we are ever the custodians. Mystics, willfully strange or scandalous characters, have always played the role of rebels within the church; and yet, what they seek is nevertheless the "unification of being," the fusion of heaven and earth. That granted, it is necessary not to be tempted by "the repose offered by Unity," Blanchot stipulates, just as it is imperative not to stop "at God any more than at God's silence or absence." There is no doubt that, in writing this, Blanchot was also referring to himself, having often been heavily criticized as too aligned with negative theology. Yet this *passion of negative thought* that he shared with Bataille is not theological; it is even, he insists, "a fierce, tireless, rejection of all religious presuppositions." Foucault would later revive this idea, exploring what he called "the thought from outside" in Blanchot's fictional work. What is the origin of this strange thought, he asked, that gives rise in Blanchot's writing, as in that of other writers of modernity, to "an unending outpouring of language" in which the speaking subject effaces itself—an experience that first appears with Sade and Hölderlin and reappears in the second half of the nineteenth century with Nietzsche and Mallarmé before flourishing in the work of Artaud, Bataille, Blanchot, and Klossowski? "One might assume that it was born of the mystical thinking that has prowled the borders of Christianity since the texts of the Pseudo-Dionysus: perhaps it survived for a millennium or so in the various forms of negative theology. Yet nothing is less certain: although this experience involves going 'outside of oneself,' this is done ultimately in order to find oneself, to wrap and gather oneself in the dazzling interiority of a thought that is rightfully Being and Speech."[24]

Neither in Bataille's nor in Blanchot's work, then, does negativity withdraw into a system, resulting in a stabilizing and soothing end. It does not conclude, writes Blanchot, in a beyond of the world "where man entrusts himself to an absolute term (God, Being, the Good, Eternity, Unity)." The same rejection—perhaps even more surprising, at least for those who simplify or ossify his thought—should also be signaled in the work of Levinas, who similarly criticizes those who seek repose from thought in theology. He strongly urges caution, as such, to anyone who would believe that the face of the other functions "as the sign of a hidden God": "thus opens the dangerous way in which a pious thought, or one concerned with order, hastily deduces the existence of God."[25]

Neither theology nor the dialectic use of negation, then. "The interior experience," writes Blanchot, "is the manner in which this radical negation, a negation that has nothing more to negate, is affirmed." A pure negativity, as it were, always open, without totality or synthesis, inexhaustible, revived ad infinitum, both faithful and unfaithful to Hegelian thought. We know the extent to which Blanchot, like many other intellectuals of his generation (Bataille, but also the early Lacan), was lastingly influenced by the lectures given by Alexandre Kojève on *The Phenomenology of Spirit* at the *École des Hautes Études* in the 1930s. It goes without saying that one of the most original contributions of Kojève's "negativist" and anthropological reading was precisely the emphasis he placed on this category that was, for him, fundamental: the *dialectical-suppression* (*Aufhebung*) as a liberating and creative force. On Kojève's interpretation, it is human existence that is dialectical, which is to say negationist or, in other words still, "creative-Action," History, Work, power of change: "And one can give an account of Man thus understood only by taking account of the negativity which he implies or realizes—that is, by describing the 'dialectical movement' of his real existence, which is the movement of a being that continues to be itself and yet does not remain the same."[26] No doubt what interested Blanchot was precisely this energy of thought that Kojève brings to the fore in Hegel's text, this "prodigious power of the negative" that he himself discussed at length in *Literature and the Right to Death.* It is the same relentless negativity Blanchot sees at work in the affirmation he considers to run through all of Nietzsche's thought: namely, that of man as "infinite power of negation."[27]

"This surplus of 'negativity,'" wrote Blanchot in his homage to Bataille, "is in us the infinite heart of the passion of thought."[28] This is, I believe, a fundamental statement, and one that must be kept in mind as we read the texts of these twentieth-century writer-thinkers if we hope to understand the link between anguish, being out of oneself, and this tireless energy of the negative that constitutes the singularity of their writings. In the end, what they confront is that which at times has been called the inhuman and at others the sublime. As we know, both terms were privileged in turn by Jean-François Lyotard, who emphasized the role played in anguish by the confrontation with the inhuman, in the sense of a power of destruction exceeding the individual, an "unpresentable" that exceeds thought. Such a paradoxical sentiment of joy and anguish, of excitation and depression, is precisely, he underlined, that which seventeenth- and eighteenth-century Europe rebaptized as the sublime.[29]

The Dishuman

This anguish of the inhuman or "dishuman" [*déshumain*] (to borrow Pierre Fédida's term) is undoubtedly best heeded by psychoanalysis, which accords to destructivity its fundamental place in the explanation of all creation—hardly a coincidence, given that psychoanalysis is a knowledge and practice that, as Foucault often noted, aims to *undo* man as traditionally defined in terms of positivity. Fédida, following Freud, accordingly puts the emphasis on the negative hallucination entailed in transference, with the word "negative," he underlines, being the sign of that which "disestablishes" [*désinstitue*] anyone undergoing analysis: reclining on the couch, I must make whoever is behind me disappear so as to be able to speak, and it is this loss, this vanishing of the person, that constitutes the analytical space and allows me to extricate myself from childhood or imaginary scenarios. During analysis, concludes Fédida, "I never truly know to whom I address myself."[30]

Even more than the central role negativity, or indeed negativism, plays in melancholy or depression, it is the eminently positive aspect of a certain type of psychic violence that is brought to light through psychoanalysis. Fédida reminds us, for example, that a depressive state characterized less by despondency or sadness than by a kind of violent distress in which excitation appears to be a survival method was already recognized within the German-language psychiatric tradition, which qualified this as a type of "agitated depression" ("*aufgeregte Depression*"; literally, "excited depression"). Moreover, Melanie Klein's, and subsequently Winnicott's, theories on the depressive position (or capacity) are equally instructive here. For what they both ultimately teach us is that not only have we all been depressed at an early stage of our lives and that this is an essential trait of the human psyche but also that depression is indispensable to the ulterior development of the capacity to play, dream, and imagine—in short, to any creative activity of thought.[31]

The writers and philosophers whom I discuss in this book are proof of the paradoxical vitality of depressive negativity. I can readily imagine that this violence was, in their case, particularly active (in the sense one speaks of a volcano's activity) and that they no doubt had to be exceptionally capable of tolerating such a destructive force before being able to transfigure this into work of thought. Far from the phobic avoidance that characterizes many contemporary normopaths and narcissists who, preferring to know nothing about it, elude all pain and take glory in the vain glimmering of inconsequential writing games for hurried readers, the authors that concern me here write in the closest proximity to depression, expose themselves to it and traverse it. In this sense, being out of oneself can also be understood as the "beside oneself" [*hors de soi*] one experiences with anger—and although sometimes unnoticed in their work, such anger bears a strong resemblance to the furor of Antiquity, which, as we know, the Ancients associated with creation. We would be wrong, for example, to overlook in the work of the gentle, civilized Blanchot the explosions of anger that marked some of his articles in the 1930s, or the (self-)aggressive darkness of a certain Beckettian laugh, the rages of Lacan and Derrida . . . We should not be at all surprised that Artaud willingly associated his Theater of Cruelty with the plague, cholera, and anger, those paradigms of a violent discharge of energy, a "formidable call to the forces," the liberation of the "compressed unconscious." Although in a much less obvious way, it is indeed a similar sublimation of destructive negativity that figures in the soft whisper of Beckett's dead voices, just as it does in the eternal vitality of ruins in his later work. As such, it is already present in *Waiting for Godot*:

> ESTRAGON: All the dead voices.
> VLADIMIR: They make a noise like wings.
> ESTRAGON: Like leaves.
> VLADIMIR: Like sand.
> ESTRAGON: Like leaves.
>   *Silence.*
> VLADIMIR: They all speak at once.
> ESTRAGON: Each one to itself.
>   *Silence.*
> VLADIMIR: Rather they whisper.
> ESTRAGON: They rustle.
> VLADIMIR: They murmur.
> ESTRAGON: They rustle.
>   *Silence.*
> VLADIMIR: What do they say?
> ESTRAGON: They talk about their lives.[32]

What I see in this allusion to an impossible death common to the work of Blanchot, Levinas, and Beckett is a similar fascination with a negative thought that upturns the anguish of death and makes of it an unresolvable incompletion (never-ending ending), infinitely rekindling the process of creation. Indeed, it is this formidable power of creation, lying at the heart of negativity, that drives the thought of these writers, who tirelessly explore that which undoes form and overwhelms identity: deconstruction (Derrida), *"undoing the work"* [*désoeuvrement*] and *disaster* (Blanchot), *unsaying* [*dédit*] (Levinas), *decreation, lit-*

erature of the unword (Beckett), Lacan's litany of "there is no . . . ," and Foucault's *end of man,* ironically overturning all finitude . . . In each instance, the act of unbinding is the same as that which attempts to tear thought from its tranquil, affirmative certainties, its categorical foundations. Levinas's writing is therefore at the heart of "the very essence of language, which consists in continually undoing its phrase by the foreword or the exegesis, in *unsaying the said,* in attempting to restate without ceremonies what has already been ill understood in the inevitable ceremonial in which the said delights."[33] Negativity understood as creative energy is therefore far from melancholic negativism, that fixation to nothingness or apathy in which the forces of being are immobilized.

Particles and Atoms

The singular strength of these works is precisely that they *surpass* anguish, with the "prodigious power of the negative" that defines the latter being turned against it and used, like a lever, to pulverize forms, thus harnessing the power of decomposition at anguish's core. Anguish is no longer, then, this coagulation of nothingness in which the absence of thought is immured. The void reveals itself accordingly for what it is: not an absence of life but an astounding swarming of energies, an infinite vibrational movement. This is what Beckett's *The Lost Ones* essentially shows us: that the void, like hell, is overpopulated. All form is an illusion, contemporary physics suggests: we evolve in the midst of a swarm of ceaselessly moving atoms; however deep we go into physical matter, all is pullulation, energetic vibration, circulation, direction, pulsation . . . nothing that resembles the classic stability of the notions of extension and substance. This is what these writers no doubt perceived better than anyone, rediscovering at the heart of their practice of writing the pre-Socratic intuitions of the structure of matter. We are provisional conglomerates of atoms, repeated Artaud, Bataille, Beckett, and the others. "We participate in all possible forms of life," insisted Artaud in Mexico, 1936:

> On our human Unconscious weighs a millennia-old atavism. And it is absurd to limit life. Some of what we have been and above all of what we *must be* lies obstinately inside stones, plants, animals, landscapes, and woods.
>
> Particles of our past and future *ego* roam through nature, where very precise universal laws work to bring them together. And *we should* look for replicas, active, nervous, even fluid replicas, in all of these disintegrating elements.[34]

There are endless instances of ancient atomist thought having been translated into poetic illumination for the twentieth century: for example, the word-flakes from which is woven the Unnamable, that "character" of Beckett's, a fleeting reincarnation of the whirlwind of atoms-letters: "I'm in words, made of words, others' words, what others, the place too, the air, the walls, the floor, the ceiling, all words, the whole world is here with me, I'm the air, the walls, the walled-in one, everything yields, opens, ebbs, flows, like flakes, I'm all these flakes, meeting, mingling, falling asunder [. . .] I'm all these words, all these strangers, this dust of words, with no ground for their settling, no sky for their dispersing [. . .] ."[35]

In *Inner Experience,* Bataille refers at length to the book by the physicist Paul Langevin, *La Notion de corpuscules et d'atomes,* published in 1934. He borrows from Langevin more than one reflection on the imperceptible interior goings-on that constitute the life of organic being (contagion of energy, current, electrical flow). "A human being is a particle inserted in unstable and tangled groups," he points out before noting that, as all notion of the fixity of the forms of self dissolves, so too anguish suddenly disappears: "The stabilized order of isolated appearances is necessary to the anguished consciousness of the torrential floods which carry it away. [. . .] From one end to the other of this human life which is our lot, the consciousness of the paucity of stability, even of the profound lack of all true stability, liberates the enchantment of laughter. As if this life suddenly passed from an empty and sad solidity to the happy contagion of warmth and of light, to the free tumult which the waters and the air communicate to one another [. . .]."[36]

An echo of Bataille's expenditure, of his laughter, is found in the promise of happiness figuring countless times in Beckett's work, as at the end of *Ill Seen Ill Said* where an incorruptible faith remains in spite of everything—a final rapture in reverse, in the suppression of nothingness, to breathe the void, to aspire to the void, this infinite life: "No. One moment more. One last. Grace to breathe that void. Know happiness."[37]

Aspiration, Inspiration

To invert aspiration into inspiration: such is the fundamental dynamic of creative anguish. All the same, we must first agree upon the meaning we should give today to this ancient notion of inspiration. Let us remember what Antonin Artaud wrote about anguish: "a kind of suction cup placed on the soul." The anguish of thinking opens up a gaping hole within being, he repeated, an aspiring, sucking void into which it risks sinking completely:

> The hideous sadness of the void,
> of the chasm in which there is nothing,
> it doesn't spirit the nothingness away,[38]

there is nothing,
it's around the chasm,
there where words withdraw,
a chasm without words,
syllable without sounds.[39]

Lacan arrived at a surprisingly similar definition in 1963 at the end of his seminar on anxiety—proof once more of the pertinence of Freud's observation crediting writers with an unconscious knowledge. Anxiety has no cause, states Lacan, but it is not without an object. It relates to the most profound and most archaic of objects, that *Thing* that refers to the first existent, to the subject's absolute Other. The mother initially occupies this place, but not exclusively. Anxiety can therefore arise alongside the risk of a sudden emergence of the real, a non-symbolizable *something* that refers to the Thing, this outside that is the first and fundamental "outside of myself." This is the case for the most primordial of anxieties, that which manifests itself in the first cry of a newborn child, who is not so much torn from this first universe as forced, in coming into the world, to give up a part of itself with which it had previously been whole. What a strange leap this is, writes Lacan, by which living beings leave their primitive milieu and emerge into the air: "Shouldn't we recognize here in this *something* the essential feature, in this radical intrusion, of something that is as Other to the living human being as the fact of passing over into the atmosphere? By emerging into this world where he must breathe, first and foremost he is literally choked, suffocated. This is what has been called trauma—there is no other—the trauma of birth, which is not separation from the mother but *the inhalation, into oneself, of a fundamentally Other environment.*"[40]

Defining anxiety in this way, Lacan effects an unprecedented transposition of Ferenczi's notion of the trauma of birth: less the horror of expulsion into an unknown world, away from the warmth of the matricial universe, than a choking, a suffocation, the invasion into the deepest recesses of being by what is at first radically foreign: the air that is breathed. Here, again, anxiety is a question of breath. *Inspiration* and *aspiration,* as we know, were once practically interchangeable; indeed, in the twelfth century, the *Book of Kings* still spoke of "divine aspiration" in the sense of inspiration. In their literal sense, both words mean to draw in air from outside, to inhale it into the lungs; they relate to respiration and breath (from *spirare*: to breathe, respire). The whispered speech [*parole soufflée*] that haunted Artaud . . .

It was Blanchot who most clearly reinvented this great theme of inspiration as modern myth, which he did through a poetic and at the same time terrifying allegory: that of the ceaseless murmuring of "eloquent immensity"; speech that, "wandering and always outside," has surrounded us from the beginning—"fresh breath of eternal rehashing." The writer alone has the task of forging an intimate relationship with this original rumbling. This incessant murmur, which "very much resembles inspiration, but [. . .] is not confused with it," is indeed that which the writer hears, makes silent, and transfigures into writing.[41] In this sense there is a true heroism proper to literature, and Blanchot highlights the danger every writer faces. Levinas recognized a similarity between this "eternal murmuring of the outside" and his own *there is* [*il y a*], which he conceptualized during the same period. But in what exactly does this experience analyzed by both writers consist? An absolute Other, outside of the individual and of which the anguishing strangeness strikes the senses first and foremost: what I see in the *there is,* what I hear in the murmured speech . . . the air that inflates the newborn's lungs. Or again, this desubjectifying experience of breathing as an opening up toward another being, to which Levinas devoted a page of truly inspired writing in *Otherwise than Being*: "The approach of the neighbor is a fission of the subject *beyond lungs,* in the resistant nucleus of the ego, in the undividedness of its individuality. It is a fission of self, or the self as fissibility [. . .]. To open oneself as space, to free oneself by *breathing* from closure in oneself already presupposes this beyond: my responsibility for the other and my *aspiration* by the other, the crushing charge, the beyond, of alterity."[42]

Each time, as though through a tear in the corporeal envelope (the "rending of the silent density," as Blanchot put it), *something* insidiously penetrates, enters by force. It is hardly surprising that it is in the work of Antonin Artaud that we find the most poignant account of the truly paranoid basis of this invasive experience.

Evoking precisely this "age-old experience of inspiration" in reference to Blanchot's book *Awaiting Oblivion,* Levinas stipulates: "To take on an exceptional gravity once one asks oneself [. . .] if *thought is not borne by a delirium deeper than thought itself.*"[43] This remark is essential if we are to understand Levinas's repeated comparison between René Descartes's idea of the infinite and the ancient understanding of poetry as breath and inspiration, found in the pre-Socratics and up to Plato and Aristotle. In each instance, he notes, it is a question of a radical experience of an outside, an absolute Other impossible to reduce to a Same, to something already understood and trusted (the reduction of the Other to the Same is, as we know, one of Levinas's fundamental criticisms of Western philosophy). Thus, for Descartes, one can only *receive* the notion of the infinite (it is put into me by God); and that which makes this idea of the infinite unique, as Levinas highlights, is that the content therefore overflows the container: the *ideatum* (the object represented in thought) exceeds the idea—thought thinks that which infinitely exceeds it. Which is to say that, with the thought of the infinite, the subject at once *thinks more than he or she is thinking.* Crucially, this presence of that which exceeds the ability to think, this force stemming from a fundamental exteriority, is similarly found, for Levinas, in Plato's analysis of delirium in the *Phaedrus.* Alongside logical, rational thought, Plato affirms the value of poetic delirium, the "winged thought" that comes from the gods. What interests Levinas in these two analyses, Plato's like Descartes's, is that both deal with a subversion of being or thought by *something* that exceeds and tears it, opening it up to an outside. The idea within me of the infinite and possession through poetic enthusiasm are not symptoms of irrationality: they designate—and this is a point Levinas emphasizes strongly—*the end of solitary thought,* that interior thought of the individual unyielding in his or her ego, cloistered in his or her "insular sufficiency."[44]

All of which equally relates to the decisive definition of inspiration with which Levinas ended *Otherwise than Being*: "[B]eing the author of what had been breathed in *unbeknownst to me,* of having received, one knows not from where, that of which I am the author. In the responsibility for the other we are at the heart of the ambiguity of inspiration."[45]

We Are Not Alone in Thinking . . .

Levinas's reflections are an invaluable guide for our attempt to explain the experience of anguish in the thought and writing of the twentieth century. Not that we need, for all that, to follow these through to their conclusion, particularly as regards the proposed ethical opening toward the

Other or quasi-theology of the Human ("the Other [. . .] resembles God," Levinas writes in *Totality and Infinity*). And yet, I do believe truly to betray Levinas's thinking, provisionally appropriating it and borrowing his voice, when I suggest the following: if the void is overpopulated, if the silence is filled with an incessant murmur, then *we are never alone in thinking, nor in writing.* What the experiments conducted by our twentieth-century writer-thinkers show is that, at the very beginning of thought, there is always an Other (at least one other) who thinks in my place, inside me, with me. I am made of this multitude of others, living and dead, present and resuscitated, real and imaginary, who continue to think and speak through me: recollections of ideas and texts, memory of language, reception of reminiscences, or the persistence and perpetuation of things read within each of us. Thought exists before me and my thinking it. It is what we sometimes take for discovery and what is in fact only rediscovery of language—what this language knows before us, better than us, and that we merely borrow from language before returning it thereto. From whom did this phrase come?

For Artaud, this crystallizes in a moment of paranoid tension: the flight of thoughts, God who continually claims to have inspired me, thought before me; God who eats the verses/vermin[46] of the poet in his "stillborn head": "There is something back of his head and over the ears of his thought. Something budding in the nape of his neck, rooted there from even before his beginning. He is the son of his works, perhaps, but his works are not of him; for whatever is of himself in his poetry has not been put there by himself but rather by that unconscious producer of life having designated him to be its poet and which he, for his part, had no role in designating."[47]

Gilles Deleuze (or Deleuze-Guattari) offers the most generously explicit interpretation: writing in the other, through the other. To say something in one's name is not to see oneself as an ego or a person, emphasized Deleuze: "Individuals find a real name for themselves [. . .] only through the harshest exercise in depersonalization, by opening themselves up to the multiplicities everywhere within them [. . .]." Together with Félix Guattari, he added, "we understood and complemented, depersonalized and singularized—in short, loved—one another. Out of that came *Anti-Oedipus* [. . .]."[48] The paradox of the Beckettian soliloquy is to give a place to this "unnamable" voice that speaks within me outside of me—is mine not mine.

The most stunningly lucid interpretation comes from Louis-René des Forêts, for whom this voice lies between inexhaustible chattering and hopeless muteness. To the perpetual question of how one can escape creative sterility and anguish about death, the response is more warped than one might at first think: it is by secretly welcoming voices among which I mix my own. The following extract—from a short story entitled, by no coincidence, "Une mémoire dé-mentielle" [A Demented Memory]—is an example of this in its nostalgia for moments of inspiration as dazzling as they are fleeting. What is it that characterizes these mo-ments? As the passage portrays, it is the quasi-Bataillean drunkenness of a communion that carries me beyond my-self, the ecstasy of a fusion in which my voice melts into those of other children in choral singing before overpow-ering them:

> When the voices soar up with sweet or acrid sonorities, upheld by the thunder of the organ, he mingles his own unrestrainedly, suddenly understanding that it is by active participation in the *ceremony* that he can best find access to what *the priest* would call *God*, to what nowa-days he can give no name to, all words being weak and inadequate to define the unique lightening-flash quality

of that revelation [. . .]. *At that moment something like a rushing wind arises and space recedes.* He feels within himself *a vast emptiness,* which is at the same time a plenitude. Impelled, further, by the unaccustomed power of the incantation whose meaning is no longer beyond his grasp, *he feels himself whirled around and as it were flung roughly out of space and time* into a world where everything is clear, where all *the painful contradictions that were rending him* seem resolved.[49]

What this long extract instantiates, in a way that is at once obvious and skillfully concealed, is precisely what inspiration *is* (to quote Levinas again: "being the author of what had been breathed in unbeknownst to me"). The italicized phrases have been taken directly from (inspired by) Antonin Artaud's description of the ritual of self-expropriation during the Mexican peyote ceremony. They belong to a text he wrote in 1943 at Rodez, "The Peyote Rite in Tarahumara Country." Des Forêts's *The Children's Room* contains many other passages secretly borrowed from Joyce's *Portrait of the Artist as a Young Man* and Artaud's *Heliogabalus,* among others. Voices foreign to his own and through which des Forêts weaves his own improper voice—a skillful act of plagiarism that could just as easily have been jubilant as it could profoundly distressing.[50]

Being No One

Once again in these texts we find symptoms of the "borderline" pathologies of the twentieth century: no voice of one's own, no fixed identity, fluctuation between anguish of the void and fear of the intrusion of the Other, between the dread of sterility and the fear of mimetism.[51] There is a faint trace of this, like a diminished echo, in the narcissistic waverings of the modern subject, who is continuously torn between two contradictory desires: *to be like everyone else* and *to be like no one else.* A summons not only to be "oneself," as Ehrenberg emphasized, but also to be unique: an original fashioning, an individual like no other; I speak in my name, defend my ideas, write like no one else (I create my "blog"). Dread of doubles, clones, standardization, industrialized reproduction of the same—"technological reproducibility" as Benjamin put it. But the opposing summons is just as significant: to be *like,* to follow fashion and styles, communities and tribes, to participate, to get involved . . .

We would be wrong to reject these modest identity concerns as trivial, to judge them without common measure with the torment faced by the writers and philosophers with whom we are concerned. They themselves wrote only by experiencing that same intensified anguish of which they no doubt revealed the underlying structure. In the end, what they invite us to consider is a different approach to identity (or disidentity), one that consists in going outside of oneself, in being neither like everyone nor like no one but rather—what is more radical still—in *being no one.* What they invented is a strange, impersonal subject through which the anguish of being is dispelled—relief, calm, sometimes even infinite joy: I am a temporary particle in an unstable whole; I am the multitude of voices that speak within me; I am even that which bears no relation to the return to self, this stabilized "myself" of an affirmed identity. Thus, at last, I write, I think—outside of myself. This is undoubtedly what these twentieth-century texts present to us: constantly shifting subjectivities, without a fixed point of enunciation, an "I without I" as Blanchot put it, "the splendour of the pronoun 'one'" according to Deleuze (a non-personal individuation), a Neuter, a de-person [*dépersonne*]. Not the madness of an absence of identity nor the stupefaction of a subject without image but the play of a rift between I and me, a hiatus kept open, allowing movement and the "free play of articulations" that Artaud admired in Balinese dancers. Thus, the writer is no longer "himself," as Blanchot said; already he is no longer anyone: "The third person is myself become no one, my interlocutor turned alien; it is my no longer being able, where I am, to address myself and the inability of whoever addresses me to say 'I'; it is his not being himself."[52]

This is almost certainly the reason for the singular form of commentary which is that of our writer-thinkers, in which the I who writes is unable to do so "in its name" except by borrowing the voice of the other, loaning his or her voice to the words of others. Hence Foucault reading Blanchot or Deleuze, Deleuze reading Foucault in his turn, Levinas commenting on Blanchot, the latter commenting successively on Foucault, Derrida, Levinas, and so on. We could go on listing ad infinitum the works in which the subjects of enunciation become dizzyingly and inextricably entwined. "Who speaks in the works of Beckett?" asked Blanchot in a commentary on *The Unnamable.* "Who speaks in Foucault's 'thought from outside?'" we might echo. Most exemplary of all are the commentaries Derrida wrote on Artaud's work: they are a brilliant demonstration of that temporary and joyous dissociation of the self through listening to the work of the other that allowed him not to write *like* Artaud but to write *himself through* Artaud's writing. The same is true of his readings of Francis Ponge and Blanchot. As a result, what we read in some of the most surprising moments of "To Unsense the Subjectile" or *Signsponge*[53] is the writing of a subject that would be Artaud-Derrida or Derrida-Ponge, just as there was Deleuze-Guattari. In the relief of no longer being "riveted to oneself," as Levinas put it—this temporary exit from the conscious and aware fixed-identity subject that is sure of knowing what it is saying when it writes—there is undoubtedly an intoxicating feeling of lightness: I temporarily abandon all right to ownership over a thought that is consequently no longer mine alone. Whence the virtuosity and the verve of these writings that flow and *fly/steal* [*volent*][54] (literally and in every sense)—as well as the risk of a sometimes overexcited exaltation, as with the euphoria of Derrida's last work, in which he sometimes exhausts himself or writes too much.

If, when reading moments like these, readers are in their turn transfixed with such wonder, this is because what they are reading is no longer merely the writing of a given individual (in this case, Jacques Derrida in 1977 or 1986),[55] but first of all the invitation to a shared experience of jubilant desubjectivation in which *I think outside of myself.*

Suffice it to say that we are far from the famous Enlightenment motto Immanuel Kant was to take up in echo of d'Alembert and Voltaire: "to think in one's own way [*penser d'après soi*]," "to think for oneself [*penser par soi-même*]." Accepting the risk of the madness of thought (madness *in* thought) is an approach characteristic of twentieth-century writing, and in it can be seen the entire evolution of modern subjectivities: an evolution that takes us from the anguish of thought to the invention of new disidentities in which is unremittingly recreated a plural yet singular subject—a temporary subject, who is fragile but also, and at the same time, persevering and resistant.

Anyone who has experienced reading the texts of which I have spoken (those of Derrida, Lacan, Levinas, Beckett, Blanchot, and others besides) will know the marvel that they can arouse and their at times vertiginous effects. Because they invent new subjects of enunciation and other positions of subjectivity, they put us *outside of ourselves*— to be understood in the sense of this being "out of oneself"[56] to which I have been alluding, this logical, rational, and transferential plasticity that we must develop in order to follow them. Each of them, to varying degrees and in unique ways, invents other forms of syntax that destabilize the relationships between words and make them move. Just as we can only view certain contemporary installations by moving ourselves with them in space ("Seeing is a dance," said Jean-François Lyotard), we can only read these texts by upending our linear conventions, by exiting the orthogonal frameworks of our thoughts, by *dissociating* ourselves from ourselves. Reading is a joy.

THE VOICES OF JACQUES DERRIDA

Listening to Writing

Of all the voices now fallen quiet that embodied what was once called *French thought,* the one that lives on within me, unique among them, is that of Jacques Derrida. We sometimes forget the extent to which he, the philosopher of arche-writing, was attentive to voices. That he denounced what he called "phonologism"—the complicity of the *phonè* (voice) and a certain metaphysics of the sign—should not overshadow the importance that listening and sonority always held for him. He emphasized on numerous occasions that the operation of "hearing-oneself-speak through the phonic substance" gives an illusion of self-presence or immediate proximity ("the living voice") that confined writing for a long time to a secondary and instrumental function: that of a simple transcription of the voice.[1] Among certain of the rhetoricians and sophists of which Plato wrote, this same illusion gave rise to an opposition between the supposed corpse-like rigidity of writing and "living" speech. This, then, is what Derrida denounces—this secondarity, this false duality. In writing, Derrida himself always heard voices. What he criticized was not the voice but *the voice without writing.*

| | | | |

From this point of view, it is worth reminding ourselves of the emphasis he placed, during one of his last interviews in the summer of 2004, on the importance of the archived voice of certain writers, and especially on the concept and dramaturgy of elocution in the case of Antonin Artaud. For him, unlike the recorded voices of other writers or philosophers whose recordings we can also listen to—Joyce, Paul Valéry, Paul Celan, and Heidegger being cited indiscriminately here by Derrida—the voice of Artaud lives on in his texts. Reading Artaud, he pointed out, should necessarily entail "that we resuscitate his voice, that we read him pronouncing his texts," or in other words that we make heard the voice of his writing. Anyone who has heard Jacques Derrida read extracts from Artaud's work (for example, in his lecture "Artaud le Moma," which he gave on several occasions) will know that he always endeavored—rightly or wrongly—to perform or theatricalize his reading, reproducing as best he could what he thought to be Artaud's diction and breath (the model being the voice of Artaud in *To Have Done with the Judgment of God*), loaning his own voice to Artaud's, pronouncing those glossolalic syllables with the force with which he thought they should be uttered. These readings sometimes left listeners feeling uncomfortable, little convinced of the necessity of attempting to imitate Artaud in this way; but was it only an attempt at imitation? In the same interview, he added the following, which is essential to understanding how, for him, voice and writing are intertwined: "Artaud's voice, [. . .] once you've heard it, you can no longer silence it. And so you have to read him with *his* voice, with the spectre, the phantom, of his voice, which you have to keep in your ear. For me, the archivization of voices is something deeply moving. Unlike photography, the archived voice is 'living.' It lives another life, such as no other archive lives. It's in the voice that we hear, as it were, the self-relationship, the auto-affection of life by itself. These few recordings of Artaud's voice are an essential part of what remains for us of his body, of the body of his work."[2]

Paradoxically, then, it is because it has fallen quiet, because it is cut off from the supposedly "living" present of its utterance, that the recorded, archived voice can be more than living: it is what *returns* like Nietzsche's eternal return—a survival (living on) that overwhelms life.[3]

Now nearly three years since the death of Jacques Derrida in October 2004, I am listening again to the recordings of our last interview, in which we discussed Artaud. I did not remember having saved the audible trace of his voice, itself now archived like those of the writers about whom he had spoken that day: Artaud, Joyce, Celan, and all the others. All those to whom he gave interviews during his last years—and there were many, given how often he spoke publicly toward the end—know to what extent his speech, however improvised it might be, was borrowed from writing. Faultless in his syntax, with no sign of familiarity, it was as though, in speaking, he were merely following the sentence he had written in the air. There was such a concentration of written form in the syntactic articulation of his speech (split clauses, the insertion of parenthetic and interpolated clauses without losing the main train of thought, the fluent use of the imperfect subjunctive and locutions of circumspection like "dare I say . . ." and "we might suppose . . .") that there was barely any need in transcription to remove marks of oral language, of spoken French. One had only to retranscribe the oral-written sentence precisely as it was, without modification, and one could hear, when rereading it, even the phrasing of his intonation, and the Mediterranean accent that sometimes returned.

He spoke to me, once again, of what he called his "youthful identification" with Artaud, whom he had discovered as an adolescent in Algeria on reading *Correspondence with Jacques Rivière,* those letters in which Artaud, a young poet recently arrived in Paris, wrote of his *impower* [*impouvoir*] and anguish of thought. Derrida felt empathetic toward this writer torn between a violent urge to write and the powerlessness to do so. This anguish, this feeling of emptiness, was, Derrida claimed, something he experienced painfully until the age of thirty (a late adolescence, he added, smiling). The most obvious manifestation of this came at the age of fifteen when he felt "protean," as though afflicted by a mimicry that forced him to adopt all appearances and all voices without ever managing to find his own: "I said to myself: I can write everything, and so I can write nothing. Here was the void that I thought I recognized in Artaud. As though I was saying to myself: at my core, I am nothing, I can be anyone, I can adopt this stance or that stance, so what is my approach, where is my voice?"[4] The struggle between this vehement desire to write (literature at first, he underlined, before even thinking about philosophy) and the inability to do so filled him with anguish and despair. He sometimes recounted the long depression he experienced at around the age of thirty (also recorded in Geoffrey Bennington's biographical note)[5]; this consisted of a period of profound exhaustion and a fear of going mad, from which he began to emerge only some two years later (he was writing at the time the introduction to Husserl's *Origin of Geometry*), and then in stages until his sudden and remarkable explosion of writing in the mid-1960s, which saw the almost simultaneous publication of his first three books (*Of Grammatology, Writing and Difference, Voice and Phenomenon*). This indefatigable fever of writing and speech was never to cease again (producing more than sixty works in forty years)—to such an extent that sometimes, in his later years, his detractors would make sarcastic remarks about the inexhaustible reserves of inspiration that led him to give innumerable lectures all over the world and publish every year some three or four books, to the great dismay of many readers, who could no longer keep up with such a pace. No doubt there is more to read in this than simply the inverse of that same symptom of powerless anguish. And yet . . .

I listen again to the recorded voice: "but today still, when I have to start writing, I find myself in the same situation: before writing, I'm absolutely not . . . , I'm . . . and even when it's a modest text, nothing important, just circumstantial, three or four pages, etc., it's *really* . . . for a short while . . . I start to write, and there . . . I experience the same thing, *mutatis mutandis,* of course . . . but before *every* text I write, there's the same blank, the same despair . . . a feeling of powerlessness [*impouvoir*]: 'I'll never be able to do it, never' . . . even for very, very small things, really very small. It hasn't left me, then. [. . .] OK, let's move on . . . what were we saying?" This time, the syntax lacks its usual fluidity.

It could be shown, I believe, that some of his first reflections on the notions of trace, the *always already* and *differance* [*différance*] are not very far removed from the question that was, for him, pivotal: that of the anguish of writing and thought. "It is because writing is *inaugural,* in the fresh sense of the word, that it is dangerous and anguishing," he writes in *Writing and Difference.*[6] The patient deconstruction of the notions of present and self-presence that he was then undertaking was to culminate in the very notion of beginning—understood according to a certain "vulgar conception of time": that of a pure chronological linearity linking the past to the present—coming undone, as would also the anguish tied to it. What his reflection on the "supplement" in relation to Freud and Rousseau shows is that every present forever differs from itself: "Everything begins with reproduction. Always already: repositories of a meaning which was never present, whose signified presence is always reconstituted by deferral, *nachträglich,* belatedly, *supplementarily* [. . .]. The call of the supplement is primary, here, and it hollows out that which will be reconstituted by deferral as the present."[7] If the origin has never been present, if the speaking subject always finds him- or herself in an irreducible secondarity[8] within the organized field of speech, or, in other words, if everything has always already begun at the moment when I believe I begin speaking in my own name, then I have two possibilities: either I founder in an anxiety of persecution and protest against the dispossession of my thought, against my speech which has been stolen from me (which is what Jacques Derrida was to read in Artaud's first letters), or I am as though instantaneously liberated, relieved of the duty of being me, a unique copy, a subject original among all, speaking without repetition or mimetism.[9] Thus, since I am no longer alone when I write, since many other voices speak inside me and I am "always already" caught up in this repetition that spirits away what I thought to be my "inaugural power" . . . , then, liberated from myself, I write.

A Mad Audacity

The revelation that allowed him to write was, then, the following: I have no voice of my own ("I am aphasic," he would say in *Monolingualism of the Other*); any voice is, by definition, improper, my own–not my own. His most singular discovery, in my opinion, was therefore the progressive invention of another system of thought, the paradoxical place of a truth that does not exclude that Other that speaks within me, the madness, the dream, the poetic writing, the dramatized deliverance of words and voices.

Were I asked to express in just a few words what the thought of Jacques Derrida meant to me, the words that come to mind would be those, now quasi-international, of *borderline* and *double bind.* Words which he himself, on more than one occasion, hijacked, turning them away from their psychiatric and psychoanalytical application to evoke the concerted confrontation of his thought with the threats of instability, the unbearable, even madness. Everything can perhaps first be glimpsed in the critique he made of Michel Foucault's reading of the first of Descartes's *Meditations,* presented in *History of Madness.* Indeed, Derrida was to show here with particularly cunning subtlety how Foucault participated in the very logic he denounced: that of a division between reason and unreason, and of an exclusion of madness. Caught in the very trap it denounced, however, Foucault's reading therefore became, paradoxically, "a powerful gesture of protection and internment." What Foucault had, indeed, either not known or not been *able* to read is that Descartes "installs the threatening possibility [of madness] at the heart of the intelligible." Further yet, Derrida discerned in *Meditations* the sign of an instability at the very heart of Cartesian thought, a fundamental disquiet as to the boundaries between wakefulness and sleep, reality and illusion, reason and madness.[10] "The hyperbolical audacity of the Cartesian Cogito," he wrote, "its mad audacity, [. . .] would consist in the return to an original point which no longer belongs to either a *determined* reason or a *determined* unreason, no longer belongs to them as opposition or alternative. Whether I am mad or not, *Cogito, sum.* Madness is therefore, in every sense of the word, only one *case* of thought (*within* thought)."[11]

| | | | |

How then are we to conceive of a space of writing that would be up to the task of a thought comprising the risk of madness and that would, in this way, deploy a wealth of creativity, infinite vitality, and unexpected inventive powers? Or again: what would thought become when it is not *bordered* by, or no longer confined by, the peaceful assurance of not being mad (or the dread of being so)? "Infinitely extending the frontiers of what we call reality," said Antonin Artaud. We know, of course, where all of this can lead. As such, the aim of the philosopher is not to thoughtlessly follow in the footsteps of poetic delirium, since there is, as we know, "method" in the madness he or she accepts. Derrida attributed to Descartes a "mad audacity." Thus understood, philosophy is indeed a form of heroism:

> the *hubris* of the prophet sent off for having had himself assigned a mission whose undecipherable letter arrives only at himself who understands it no better than anyone else, save for that very fact, the despair of the innocent child who is by accident charged with a guilt he knows nothing about, the little Jew expelled from the Ben Aknoun school, for example, or the drug-factor incarcerated in Prague, and everything in between, and here he is bending beneath the burden, he takes it on without taking it on, nervous, worried, hunted, cadaverized like the beast playing dead and melding with the foliage, literature in short, to escape the murderers or their pack, cadaver carrying himself, heavy like a thing but light so light, he runs he flies so young and light futile subtle agile delivering to the world the very discourse of this impregnable inedible simulacrum, the theory of the parasite virus, of the inside/outside, of the impeccable *pharmakos*, terrorizing the others through the instability

> he carries everywhere, one book open in the other, one
> scar deep within the other, as though he were digging the
> pit of an *escarre* in the flesh [. . .].[12]

At least some part of Derrida's reflection on boundaries, limits, divisions, and border crossings (a reflection that is at once and inextricably philosophical, ethical, and political) is anchored in this line of thought. Thus, he struggled tirelessly to conceptualize an anteriority outside of chronology that would give rise to oppositions without being taken up in them, just like—although any such likeness is impossible—the *khôra,* that unfigurable figure of the origin in Plato's *Timaeus.*[13] *Khôra*: another name for *space, trace, differance,* those concepts inscribed at the very heart of mad paradoxes. For it is indeed a question of bringing writing and reflection to the very place of the untenable, of the destabilizing paradox: precisely that same paradoxical *double bind* that—as the anti-psychiatrists of the 1960s put it—risks driving those who confront it mad. This is equally the case with those unrepresentable topological structures in which the part is larger than the whole, or those "undecidable" figures that were, later on, the *returned* announcing the to-come [*à venir*] *qua specters* neither living nor dead, neither present nor absent, etcetera: paradoxical actors in the theater of Derridean thought. What he calls again in poetico-philosophic terms "predicates that are contradictory or incompatible between themselves, in their very *between,* in their interlacing."[14]

This "mad audacity" was no doubt also that of our writers of modernity, to whom Derrida is, in many ways, so close; those who, like Beckett, Joyce, Artaud, and Blanchot, explored, for their part, the space of literature, "where truth lacks," as Blanchot wrote. "This is the essential risk. Here we reach the abyss."[15] And, as in these writers' work, perhaps, there is the same undecidability of laughter and tears, of joy and sadness, of despair and *jouissance*—an extraordinary pleasure of language and words that permeates and stirs the suffering. Derrida's speaking and thinking "in tongues" is not as far as one might think from these modern literary epiphanies. For him as for them, it is less about the invention of terms than of a paradoxical syntax that places words in a precarious balance and opens them up like sentences to a multiplicity of meanings in suspense. Take for example the word "knowledge [*savoir*]"—a philosophical word if ever there were one—in Hélène Cixous's text, where Derrida deciphers "*ça*," "*sa*," "*s'avoir*," and so on: "the unique body of an unheard-of word, more or less than a word, the grammar of a syntagm in expansion. A sentence in suspense that flaps its wings at birth[. . .]."[16] Discourse in suspense, text in an infinite process, like that, too, of a certain work by Freud (*Beyond the Pleasure Principle*), in which Derrida discerns a nonpositional structure, "strategies of approach and overflow, strictures of attachment or of mooring, places of reversion, strangulation, *double bind.* These are constitutive of the very process of the athesis [. . .]."[17] *Athesis*: to be understood as the impossibility to fix, limit, or *border* the thesis in an *in-itself* without *beyond.* "That's what they can't stand, that I say nothing, never anything tenable or valid, no thesis that could be refuted, neither true nor false, not even, not seen not caught, it is not a strategy but the violence of the void through which God goes to earth to death in me, the geologic program, me, I've never been able to contradict myself, that's saying, so I write, that's the word [. . .]."[18] He wrote, that's the word.

Biography, Belongings

It must be acknowledged, Derrida proposed, that between literature and philosophy there is a *partage* [sharing, division, distribution], in every sense of the word, which also implies "some new and rigorous distinctions, a complete re-distribution of spaces."[19] The philosophical theater of writing and voices that constitutes Derrida's oeuvre can there-fore also be understood as a fundamental reflection on the frontiers between the voice that is supposedly one's own (its link to the biographical) and the public voice. Writing about Nietzsche, for example, his examination of what we call "the life of a philosopher" was to dwell particularly on the *dynamis* of this strange "divisible border" between the philosopher's work and life that runs through both "bod-ies" (the *corpus* and the biological body [*corps*]), this un-tenable position, at once both auto- and allo-biographical, that nevertheless allows them to write. Nietzsche is more-over, he underlines, someone who treated philosophy "with his name, in his name"—to the very extent, no doubt, that he learned "to pluralize in a singular fashion the proper name."[20] Accordingly, it is no coincidence that the articula-tion of the private and public spheres was at the center of his final reflection—what those on the other side of the At-lantic were sometimes too quick to call the *political turn* of Jacques Derrida. We can certainly see more than a friendly nod to Blanchot's political reflections on community and belonging in *Parages,* when Derrida reads the *genou* [knee] of *La Folie du Jour*'s female "protagonist" as *je/nous* [I/us].[21]

What does "to belong" mean? This is a question that ap-pears time and again, in one form or another, throughout Derrida's work. The question is posed anew in many areas of contemporary thought, including philosophy, literature or, more broadly, the social sciences. Behind it lies just as much a desire to examine current identity tensions as the challenging of any idea of belonging, whether linguistic, national, communitarian, or sexual. No doubt it is neces-sary to draw parallels between these "tensions" and "chal-lenges" insofar as they are two sides of the same symptom.

In this perspective, the question posed across many of Derrida's texts is twofold at the least. Firstly, what remains of our belongings that, in a certain sense and no doubt in many ways, *held us together*? This interrogation is incontestably nostalgic but, in a larger sense, it covers the issue of shared meaning and community. Secondly, must we try to reinvent new forms of belonging? And under what conditions? With what limits? This time the question concerns the *future-to-come* [*l'à-venir*], as he used to say, and, even more fundamentally, the meaning to be given to all works, whether literary or philosophical—works of art or works of life. And no doubt Jacques Derrida intended to make his life *also* a work of art—a fantasy that, as we know, is not only that of writers.

As always, or nearly always, we can identify within Derrida's texts a seemingly contradictory double attitude. On the one hand there is a refusal of belonging in the sense of identity, assimilation, the proper [*propre*], oneself, and so on. So familiar are these themes in his philosophy that Geoffrey Bennington refers to his "impatience with gregarious identification, with the militancy of belonging in general": "this difficulty with belonging, one would almost say of identification, affects the whole of J.D.'s oeuvre, and it seems to me that 'the deconstruction of the proper' is the very thought of this."[22] Yet, on the other hand, there is the necessity to belong. Here, we must remind ourselves, for example, of the analyses he dedicates in *Monolingualism and the Other* to the risks of collapse or tension that can result from a refusal or an impossibility to belong: "The break with tradition, uprooting, [. . .] amnesia, indecipherability, and so on: all of these unleash the genealogical drive, the desire of the idiom [. . .]. The absence of a stable model of identification for an ego—in all its dimensions: linguistic, cultural, and so on—gives rise to impulses that are always *on the brink* of collapse[. . .]."[23]

In this sense, as we can see, for Derrida belonging is both impossible and necessary. It is, at once and interchangeably, "I refuse but also I cannot" (because the question is not a simple one; it is just as theoretical as it is deeply painful). We are reminded of that beautiful phrase in "Circumfession": "who am I if I am not what I inhabit and where I take place?"[24] I shall return later to the question of place, but I would first like to make a detour via another example: that of Derrida's reflection on Europe, or, as we say, the European *Community*, in *The Other Heading*. This book, as we know, was originally a contribution to a colloquium on "European cultural identity" held in Turin in 1990. In it, he investigates precisely this question of belonging, or not belonging, to a supposed European identity. What does it mean to be a European philosopher, he asks, when what one tries to invent is another approach to identity and discourse, consisting in the paradoxical gesture of at once gathering oneself together in difference with oneself and opening oneself up, without being able any longer to gather oneself together? Does that mean, for example, embodying all by oneself that permanent crisis of the European spirit already evoked by Paul Valéry?

One of Jacques Derrida's most significant hypotheses was precisely to try to conceive of another topology, another relation to space and to set theory—an *a priori* paradoxical topology, where, for example, the part would be larger than the whole and the outside would also be inside. Here is what he concluded at the end of *The Other Heading*: "I am European, I am no doubt a European intellectual, and I like to recall this [. . .]. But I am not, nor do I feel, European *in every part*. [. . .] Belonging as 'fully a part' should be incompatible with belonging 'in every part.' My cultural identity, that in the name of which I speak, is not only European, it is not identical to itself." And a little further on: "If, to conclude, I declared that I feel European *among other*

45

things, would this be, in this very declaration, to be more or less European? Both, no doubt."[25] There is no need to insist upon the subtle difference he introduces here between "belonging as fully a part" [*appartenance à part entière*] and "belonging in every part" [*appartenance de part en part*]. Beyond the play on words (*appartenir, la part, le parti, la partie,* etc.), this is a matter of distinguishing between "belonging as fully a part" (i.e., without restriction) and "belonging in every part" (i.e., completely, in assembling all the parts or portions without *any remainder* [*sans reste*]). What he is saying, then, is that he is *unrestrictedly* European but not *totally.* So what does it mean to be at once more than European and less than European? It is to renounce the "in every part," the totality of belonging; it is to try to hold that seemingly untenable paradox of a belonging penetrated by heterogeneity and dissemblance, and to create from this thought and writing—which is to say, thought *in* writing. Indeed, only such a belonging is capable of *holding together,* in the fragile balance of a precarious composition, the contradictory forces of paradox that forever threaten to fix themselves in binary opposition.

To truly understand this Derridean definition of belonging, which in the end seems to make perfectly good sense (after all, who could declare themselves "European in every part"?), we must, I believe, relate it to what, beyond the real, has always been, for him, a fantasy of strangeness or foreignness. Here one may recall a remark he made during a colloquium organized in Montreal in 1979, which Régine Robin brought up again recently, a remark that, she said, certainly did not go unnoticed. During the discussion, Derrida was to say: "If I am not mistaken, none of the subjects around this table has French as their mother tongue, except perhaps the two of us, and even then, *you* are French (referring to the psychoanalyst François Peraldi), I'm not. I'm from Algeria . . ."[26] This remark was all the more intriguing, says Régine Robin, insofar as, for the Quebecois academics present, Derrida undoubtedly epitomized Frenchness in its most traditional sense. It is this fantasy—of belonging without belonging, of being French but not "in every part"—that clearly we must analyze. A fantasy, however, is not necessarily an illusion.

Here, we must consider the "disorder of identity" he often evoked in relation to himself, which is to say quite simply that this disorder is one he suffered from: "To be a Franco-Maghrebian, one 'like myself' is not [. . .] a surfeit or richness of identities [. . .]. In the first place, it would rather betray a *disorder of identity* [*trouble d'identité*]."[27] The following biographical facts, which he himself often recounted, are well known: the despair of having been, as he wrote in "Circumfession," "the little Jew expelled from the Ben Aknoun school" in Algiers following the abolition, in October 1940, of the Crémieux decree that had granted French nationality to Algerian Jews since 1870. This "excision of citizenship" was to last two years, and he spoke on more than one occasion of his suffering and inconsolable mourning at having been so brutally marked as a foreigner, excluded and outside the community. This is also the source of the untenable position he sought to assume throughout his entire life: to be French without being French, speaking a language that was not his own. "I have only one language, yet it is not mine,"[28] he wrote. Like everyone, no doubt, but precisely more profoundly and painfully than everyone. We could add to this non-exhaustive list of personal paradoxes that forged his "disorder of identity" the fact of being Jewish without Judaism, which is perhaps what explains his kinship—not to say strange identification—with Freud, which led him on occasion to suggest that deconstruction was a form (secular? non-orthodox?) of psychoanalysis.

| | | | |

I referred earlier to a fantasy of strangeness or foreignness in Jacques Derrida's work. Fantasy, here, must be understood as an imaginary scenario, a genuine psychical elaboration or creation that no doubt allowed him to invent the singular form of his thought, his proper (and improper) idiom. Here, fantasy is a schema of thought; it is the plastic and paradoxical form that gradually "gave place to" his thought[29]—an untenable, atopic place, as he often underlined, but a place nevertheless. A place or a theater, a *scene* of writing where it was possible to play out the complex desire to be at once both here and elsewhere, outside and inside, at the center and at the margins, French and foreign, neither one nor the other, and so on; thinking and writing in a language that includes the language and thought of the other, and hence allowing him to be that philosopher precariously balanced above the void who was to prompt us to think, at the same time, by a stroke of genius unique to him, the identity flaws and anxieties of an age. Our age, still today. Derrida was, as we know, someone who was never able to belong to anything . . . or at least not for very long: no group, no institution, no place of power. In this sense, he is the opposite of Michel Foucault, who firmly established himself at the very heart of academic and publishing institutions. No doubt it was not a matter of exactly the same dissidence in the case of one and the other. We can, in any case, reread in this light the regularly recurring term *belonging* [*appartenance*] in Derrida's work. "That which no longer *belongs*. . . ," he wrote readily, for example—with this sentence then being completed in a number of ways: that which no longer belongs to the reason/unreason dualism, to the opposition between speech and writing, between form and meaning, etc. "A secret doesn't belong [. . .]," he stated in *The Gift of Death,* or again, in an interview on

Paul Celan, "Language doesn't belong."[30] In this "belonging without belonging" we again find that "X without X" logic that he himself remarked more than once in Blanchot's work: "death without death, speech without speech, being without being, name without name, self without self . . ."[31]

What he developed in his writing was, then, a paradoxical and *disfigured* topology of the notion of belonging, which would be something like the antidote (or perhaps *pharmakon*) to our old, worn-out notions of being-together [*être-ensemble*]. As everyone knows—and without necessarily being well versed in mathematics (any more than Derrida was, in any case)—*belonging* is also a mathematical trope relating to set theory, which is concerned with the rules governing the inclusion and exclusion of elements in a collection of objects. According to the law of the excluded middle that underpins this theory, an element *a* cannot *at once* belong and not belong to the set *S*. Equally, the element is, by definition, smaller than the set to which it belongs—since it is *inside.* Yet, in the paradoxical topology Jacques Derrida explored from his very first texts, motifs such as the supplement, trace, fold, hymen, and so on, undermine the stability of these relationships of inclusion and belonging. For him, the part can be bigger than the whole, the element larger than the set (as with the notion of *double invagination* in "The Double Session," focusing on Mallarmé, then later in *Parages,* in relation to Maurice Blanchot)—just as an element can be at once both included and excluded, neither here nor elsewhere, rejecting thereby all stability of the notions of limit, of outside and inside. Frontiers and borders become problematic as a result.

For example, in one of his final works, dealing with the archived material of Hélène Cixous who had just bequeathed her drafts and manuscripts to the French National Library, Derrida explored that logic of writing and thought he called "a crazy topology." What is this place, he asked, that claims to hold the corpus, the body, of a writer? Is a writer's body archivable? Does it not exceed the whole that claims to contain it? "The atopic, crazy (in Greek, *atopos* also means 'mad,' 'extravagant') topo-logic, the unthinkable geometry of a part bigger than that of which it is part, of a part more powerful than the whole, of a sentence out of proportion with the *what* and the *who* of that which contains it and whoever comprehends it, the atopia and the aporia of an apparently atomic element which includes in its turn, within itself, the element that overflows it and with which it sparks a sort of chain reaction, a veritable atomic explosion [. . .]."[32]

And so the philosophical scene becomes, perhaps, something other than a *huis clos*—and we know how interested Jacques Derrida was in questions of theater and architecture, those places of invention of other dimensions of space. There is no need to insist upon the logic that also emerges here of travel and infinite *"destinerrance,"* that movement *of* and *in* space that makes any inclusion of the subject impossible—whether as a matter of englobement or exclusion. But does that necessarily signify the end of any notion of belonging as the possibility of *being part* of the same whole, of the same community? How, faced with these paradoxical redefinitions of belonging that he constantly sought, do we develop a new politics of being-together? To pose this final question is, perhaps, a way of helping us imagine what we might, not "do with" Derrida's thought (in the instrumental sense), but rather continue to think in his company. I mean this in the sense that, at the beginning of *Specters of Marx,* he imagines someone approaching and saying, "I would like to learn to live. Finally. [. . .] To learn to live *with* ghosts, in the upkeep, the conversation, the company [. . .] of ghosts."[33] And, as he so amply showed, the phantom, the specter, the *revenant,* is not necessarily mournful or melancholic.

We must, then, rethink with him a new relationship between the private and public spheres that takes into account that logic of unstable borders he so often highlighted; and we must do this knowing precisely that all spheres brim over their perimeters, open and disseminate themselves, and contaminate that which, in the other, believed itself protected by its own borders. He recalled readily, as we know, that all philosophers are first and foremost living subjects, that each has a private life, a subjectivity, and a body. This point was made very clear (consciously intended and accepted) in the American documentary entitled *Derrida* (2003), in which he can be seen getting his hair cut at the hairdresser's and eating in his kitchen at Ris-Orangis. Such a stance was perhaps somewhat excessive, and it is understandable that there were accusations of narcissistic indulgence (although Derrida's self-display in this instance was, in fact, anti-narcissistic!); it nevertheless remains a fundamental demonstration of the fact that all thought is incarnated in a body. *Mutatis mutandis,* one could for that matter advance that, just as Freud maintained that the sexual drive forms the basis of every sublimated act, so Derrida showed that triviality forms the basis of every thought, however brilliant it may be. That his philosophy could put his life on show (and withstand the risks this entailed) is perhaps also testimony to its strength.

That said, between the singular and the collective there is, for Derrida, precisely a *between* [*entre*] that sets them in motion, deforms and undoes them, and causes them to infiltrate each other, thus prohibiting them from stabilizing themselves face to face like two distinct entities. There is, for example, that strange figure between the singular and the collective that he calls the specter or *revenant* or the ghost. The specter is neither private nor public; it is one and the other and always double. Crossing the boundaries between personal and collective, it is at once the bereaved memory of my own deaths (the ghost of Hamlet's father returning to haunt him) and the infinite horde of *revenants* from all the wars, exterminations, and acts of oppression and violence—just like the specter of communism that returned to haunt *Specters of Marx.* He invites us "to learn to live *with* ghosts, in the upkeep, the conversation, the company, or the companionship, in the commerce without commerce of ghosts," but what should we understand by this? "No *being-with* the other," he continues, "no *socius* without this *with* that makes *being-with* in general more enigmatic than ever for us."[34] It seems to me that all Derrida's thought here is a reelaboration of the very idea of community and belonging. It is no longer a matter of a "being together" of the community, as it was for Jean-Luc Nancy and Blanchot, but a "being with." And with whom is it about being? With a shadow, an other who is not, who is no longer or who is not yet. Someone passing [*passant*] (passed away [*trépassé*]) between life and death, and who has returned. So what is it ultimately about? Taking into account a density, an infinite complexity, of that which we were perhaps too quick to call a community, as though such a whole comprised only those present, the living, the numerable and countable elements in their being-there here and now. The conclusion of *Specters of Marx* is therefore as follows: one must learn to live *with* the ghost "by learning not how to make conversation with the ghost but how to talk with him, with her, how to let them speak or how to give them back speech, even if it is in oneself, in the other in oneself: they are always *there,* specters, even if they do not exist, even if they are no longer, even if they are not yet. They give us to rethink the 'there' as soon as we open our mouths [. . .]."[35] No longer, then, "being together" but "being with"; no longer "belonging" (in a logic of place, of being-there, of the relationship between the whole and the part) but "upkeeping" [*entretenir*], holding between [*tenir entre*], mutually maintaining, still holding him or her in life just as he or she is already holding me in death. The ghost, the one who no longer belongs anywhere but haunts everywhere, is perhaps, then, another figure of the philosopher balanced or suspended above the void, fantasizing himself here and there, outside and inside, dead and alive, always *living on* [*sur-vivant*], clinging to the untenable, the unthinkable. No doubt this is what he also proposes to us: to exit the axiomatic of self and a place of one's own [*chez soi*] (what both he and Levinas call *ipseity,* that is the re-appropriating regathering of self). There is, then, no longer a house but something of the *Unheimliche* dwelling within.[36]

This is also the disposition of the *omphalos* that he deciphers in Nietzsche's work: that of an umbilical cord that links us—a motif at once terrifying and beautiful—to the ear and mouth of an always-dead living father: "The person emitting the discourse you are in the process of teleprinting in this situation does not himself produce it: he barely emits it. He reads it. Just as you are ears that transcribe, the master is a mouth that reads, so that what you transcribe is, in sum, what he deciphers of a text that precedes him, and from which he is suspended by a similar umbilical cord."[37]

EMMANUEL LEVINAS'S
SEED OF FOLLY

I am obedient as to an order addressed to me. Such an order throws a "seed of folly" into the universality of the ego.

—Emmanuel Levinas, *Otherwise than Being*

Philosophical Poetics?

Emmanuel Levinas never hid his interest in what he himself called "mad," "unbalanced," extravagant—or even, at times, "extra-vagant"—thoughts. Recall the question he posed in *Of God Who Comes to Mind*: "does not philosophy itself consist in treating 'mad' ideas with wisdom [. . .]?"[1] Remember, too, the "mad thought of escape" in his work *On Escape*[2]: that challenge to the laws of logic and the fatality of "enchained" man, riveted to his body yet trying to "escape himself" into an impossible outside. It may be—this is at least one of the hypotheses I wish to examine here—that Emmanuel Levinas's thought is not only an exploration of thought's utmost limits but also an invitation to venture into the very heart of a thought that is methodically mad. This being the case, he is situated, far more firmly than is sometimes believed, at the core of the fundamental interrogations pursued by that modern writing Maurice Blanchot was to call, along with Bataille, the writing of "limit-experience."

Hence, for example—and the example, naturally, has not exactly been selected at random—this sentence from the first pages of *Otherwise than Being*,[3] in a section dedicated to subjectivity: "The task is to conceive of the possibility of a break out of essence" (*OB*, 8). Noting that essence in Levinas's work is to be understood, of course, as *being* [*être*] in distinction to *beings* [*étant*], what might well then signify "the possibility of a break out of essence"? Such a clearly vertiginous proposition prompts Levinas to query: "[break out] to go where? Toward what region? To stay on what ontological plane?" Above all, he asks what must be done in order that such a proposition not be collapsed back into a mere thematic—into what he calls the "betrayal of the Said." Is it necessary to invent a language? What Levinas writes in response to this is astonishing when you know of his reticence in respect of Nietzsche: might we not, he asks, have to find "a type of writing, of committing oneself with *the world, which sticks like ink to the hands that push it off* [my emphasis]?" "One should," he continues, "have to go all the way to the nihilism of Nietzsche's poetic writing, reversing irreversible time in vortices, to the laughter which refuses language." This is a hypothesis he proposes alongside others and one that he does not refuse outright. One may therefore wonder what exactly might be this poetic writing that Levinas invents in order to detach (oneself) from the world in a gesture similar to the going out of oneself that is also the objective of Blanchot's fictional and critical writing.

The fact remains that the fundamental question posed here by Levinas (in what language does philosophy speak?) reappears at the end of the same work, such that it is easy to imagine the astonishment of readers used to a more logically structured philosophical discourse—one that strives to formulate a thought clearly and unambiguously—when faced with a proposition such as that which arises in the last pages of *Otherwise than Being*: "Language *would exceed the limits of what is thought,* by suggesting, letting be understood without ever making understandable" (169, my emphasis). Here, we touch on one of the fundamental axioms of what I would willingly call Levinasian poetics: not, then, "the logical definition of the concept" but a language in which, as in poetic or prophetic speech (the poetic or prophetic *said,* to reintroduce the distinction he makes between *Said* and *Saying*), "the said remains an *insurmountable equivocation,* where meaning [. . .] does not compose a whole" (*OB,* 170; my emphasis). What Levinas was attempting would then be to invent a practice of philosophical speech that does not dismiss as improper to the expression of thought a certain poetic or prophetic said. And which, moreover, would be thought itself. The difference between the Levinas of *Totality and Infinity* and that of *Otherwise than Being* is perhaps due to his finding the otherwise saying able to think an otherwise than being.

Levinas's language, his highly distinctive syntax, is perhaps not as different as it would initially seem from that of Mallarmé, for example. "Everything is suspended, an arrangement of fragments," writes Mallarmé, the word making itself "the center of vibratory suspense, break [*brisure*] . . . disseminated."[4] *Break* and *suspense*: these are terms one cannot help but relate to the discursive practice of cuts [*coupure*] in Levinas's work, the resulting fractures being equally probed by Jacques Derrida when he pointed out how the writing of *Otherwise than Being* proceeds by a strange logic of dislocation or interruption, introduced by the trace as it tears textual tissue.[5] *Dislocation* and *interruption* in Levinas's work, *break* and *suspense* in Mallarmé's: in both cases, it is that which disturbs writing and unsettles the order of speech that we must consider. What, in fact, Levinas seeks to achieve—particularly in *Otherwise than Being*—is set down unambiguously as "confounding philosophical language." For clarity, the sentence is best cited in its entirety: "The *exceptional words* by which the trace of that which has passed and the extravagance of the approach are said—One, God—become *terms, reenter into the vocabulary* and are put at the disposition of philologists, instead of *confounding philosophical language*" (169, my emphasis).[6] We could digress here to discuss at length this single phrase "the trace of *that which has passed* [*la passée*]"; *la passée*: a quasi-portmanteau word combining *le passé* [past] and *la pensée* [thought], the trace of that which has passed into thought and continues to fade in passing. While this could perhaps be considered an obsession of mine ("obsession," as we know, is an eminently Levinassian term), I see several points in common between Levinas's reflection on language and that of Antonin Artaud. Take, for example, what Levinas says here: "The exceptional words become *terms,* reenter into the vocabulary"; this bears more than a passing resemblance to Antonin Artaud's "Letters on Language," the letters he addressed to Jean Paulhan in 1933. In these, he reflects on the invention of a new language that is a *living* language, a language of breath, of respiration, of diction. Written words are "frozen," "ossified" words, Artaud repeats, adding: "A word thus understood has little more than a discursive, i.e. elucidative, value. And it is not an exaggeration to say that in view of its very definite and limited *terminology* the word is used only to sidestep thought; it encircles it, but *terminates* it; it is only a conclusion."[7] For both Levinas and Artaud, if the word becomes a term, it is no longer anything other than an ending, the cessation of thought.

What I want to propose is not only that thought, for Levinas, is bordered by madness—to me, this seems affirmed and beyond doubt—but also that he explores in his writing, as methodical as it is inspired, domains that are similar to those explored by Artaud and other modern writers. The question is therefore not one of madness but rather, I believe—borrowing his syntax—that of exploring an "*otherwise than being*". . . *mad,* which he has in common with Antonin Artaud, among others. It is in any case this view that guides my reading of Emmanuel Levinas's work, and particularly some of his most challenging, most "unsettling" texts, such as *Otherwise than Being,* which I thereby approach from a relative familiarity with twentieth century texts considered mad or almost "unreadable": namely, those texts on the experience of limits and being out of oneself that include those by Artaud and Joyce, Blanchot's fictional writing, the later Beckett, and the works of Lacan and Derrida. In other words, I come to Levinas's work having had a certain amount of experience with destabilizing texts and that unassertive, unstable, writing that Beckett calls the writing of "decreation," or, as I am trying to portray it, the writing of *disfiguration* [*défiguration*]. It should be noted that what Emmanuel Levinas writes on the face is also to be understood as disfiguration, with the provisional and fragile figures he describes alternating incessantly between decreation and recreation.[8] In *Totality and Infinity,* for example, he writes that the face, "still a thing among things, *breaks through the form* that nevertheless delimits it." A little further on, he continues: "The permanent openness of the contours of its form in expression imprisons *this openness which breaks up form* in a caricature."[9]

What I'm proposing, then, runs contrary to the conformist, even traditionalist (religious or not) reading to which Levinas tends at times to be confined. Indeed, contrary to all such readings that tend to *thematize* his writing, imprisoning it in a *said* (a tendency from which he himself is not entirely immune when, for example, he speaks of the fables that one tells "to children and women," or he evokes the bond between father and son, forgetting the daughter), it is the wrenching force of his Saying that I am proposing to make heard, his proximity to certain texts of modernity reputed to be mad, his sometimes unnoticed kinship with the force of disfiguration—the "disidentifying" force of a certain number of modern works.

Writings on Delirium

We know just how remarkable a reader Levinas was of Maurice Blanchot; this was not only because of their long-standing friendship but no doubt more profoundly because of their psychic and intellectual proximity (with the word "psychic" here not to be understood in the particular sense Levinas gave to it, which is a point to which I shall return later). In one of the articles he dedicates to Maurice Blanchot, "The Poet's Vision" (1956), Levinas highlights the following: "Blanchot determines writing as a *quasi-mad structure* in the general economy of being, by which being is no longer an economy, as it no longer possesses, when approached through writing, any abode—no longer has any interiority."[10] This sentence is fundamental; it poses the question of how to be and how to write without inhabiting. Levinas explains how Blanchot unlocks writing for us as a "quasi-mad structure" in the sense that, as he clarifies a little later, "literature [. . .] lets out onto the unthinkable." One cannot help but be reminded here of what Antonin Artaud wrote in 1946 to his friend Marthe Robert, a translator of Kafka among others: "And the unthinkable is also a being which one day will replace thought."[11] For it is indeed, in my view, the recurring question of *how, through writing, can the unthinkable be touched upon* that the thought of these twentieth-century thinkers—writers and philosophers—precisely pursues.

Ten years later, in 1966, in another article dedicated to Blanchot, "The Servant and Her Master," Levinas raises the question of whether the experience of inspiration or possession through writing that Blanchot recounts in *Awaiting*

Oblivion would not bring us into contact with a primordial experience of language, and whether "thought [is] not borne by a *delirium deeper than itself.*"[12] Blanchot would invent here then, according to Levinas, a "discontinuous and contradictory language of scintillation"; he would undo "the structures of language," and we are perhaps wrong, Levinas says, to call "art and poetry" this "exceptional event" that "liberates language from its servitude with respect to the structures in which the *said* maintains itself."[13] Indeed, as Levinas writes again, this time in 1975 in a final article dedicated to Blanchot's truly mysterious, enigmatic *The Madness of the Day,* "the significance Blanchot attributes to literature challenges the arrogance of philosophical discourse—that englobing discourse, capable of saying everything, *including its own failure.*"[14] Philosophy is, in fact, states Levinas in a remark that would well merit further reflection, infinitely *easier to integrate into the space of the world* than literature (or what we designate as such). "It is impossible," he says, "to annex to the world this excluded middle, of which literature would be the incredible modulation. It is absolutely set apart."[15] As we know, Levinas highlights more than once the alliance between philosophical discourse, the State, and (somewhat oddly) medicine that aims at overcoming the ruptures of discourse in order to mend the "rendings of the logical text" (*OB,* 170). What Levinas denounces here, as does Blanchot, is, then, the complicity between the State ("which excludes, through violence, subversive discourse") and a certain philosophical discourse he qualifies as "coherent," "entirely absorbed in the Said." Philosophy is, as a result, at the service of order, and Levinas's tone here recalls that of Blanchot in *The Madness of the Day,* denouncing language being used in such a way that it is no longer "questioning but interrogatory [*interrogation mais interrogatoire*]." Here, we must reread the last lines of the text Levinas wrote on Maurice Blanchot's

The Madness of the Day: "The ophthalmologist and the psychologist check vision and thought; they check and they spy upon you. In their helping objectivity they are the accomplices to order, i.e. the established order. They prompt you to tell the story, to adopt the mode of existence that can be resumed in the fable—excluding the extra-vagant. Logical order is re-established by an order. The invitation to narrate is a summons. [. . .] To tell a story, to speak, is already to make a police report."[16]

One might note in passing that this is exactly what Beckett says in *Molloy* when he introduces the messengers of a mysterious and no doubt policing god who demand that people write reports for them: "tell me the story of your life . . ." And then, in *The Unnamable,* there is that strange concealed "master" who ceaselessly demands that he be given the official report of history: "It's all a bubble, we've been told a lot of lies, he's been told a lot of lies, who he, the master, by whom, no one knows, the everlasting third party . . ."[17] Now, all the philosophical and poetic work Levinas progressively elaborated over the years precisely aims at destabilizing being, the verb "to be," its definition and our use of it. He points clearly to this fundamental evolution in *Difficult Freedom,* writing: "The ontological language, which *Totality and Infinity* still uses in order to exclude the purely psychological significance of the proposed analyses, is henceforth avoided."[18] And it is the entire language that then *moves,* literally setting itself in motion and wresting itself from stability, from the repose it was afforded by existing in its being. And from then on, within the Said, as Levinas puts it, comes the call of the unsaid. Indeed, as he highlighted, for example, in his lectures at the Sorbonne published as *God, Death, and Time,* throughout the entire Western tradition "meaningful thought is thetic": "It thinks what is posited (to think is to posit), and it thinks the repose of what posits itself. This rest or repose, which is fundamental [. . .] is expressed by the verb 'to be.' [. . .] The identity of beings thus comes from a profound and fundamental experience, which is also an experience of the fundamental, the profound, and the foundation. That repose is an experience of being *qua* being—it is the ontological experience of the firmness of the earth."[19]

The challenge thereby contained in language and to which one must rise is precisely to no longer say anything that is "the same," that is simply posited or affirmed in its being. The result is a sort of uprooting of being. More than a fault or rift, which might immediately (or "mediately," we might say) turn itself inside out, close up or become dialecticized, this is a tremor in language. I have actively avoided the word "shudder," as this not only risks being taken as a Barthesian affectation but fails to capture the veritable earthquake (far more than a "shuddering") that is involved here. Let us not forget that what is required is precisely to "confound language," to never allow language or the reader to rest. Writing is thus a dizziness; and reading, a sailing on the high seas. As Levinas puts it: "movement going from said to unsaid in which the meaning shows itself, eclipses and shows itself. In this *navigation* the element that bears the embarkation is also the element that submerges it and threatens to sink it" (*OB*, 181; my emphasis).

If everything moves then, both in Levinas's thought and his language, it is because the *terra firma* ultimately gives way, and being that is riveted to itself opens into "otherwise than being," just as subjectivity opens into the "Other-in-the-Self." Thus, everything becomes movement, breathing, animation. To the stability of being and, indeed, *ethos* understood as "abode or dwelling place" in the terms of Heidegger's *Letter on Humanism,* Levinas counterposes infinite movements of contraction and rupture,[20] of inspiration and expiration, constriction and expulsion. Hence, in *Otherwise than Being*, Levinas defines "oneself," or ipseity, as a pluralized identity, constantly shifting, continually contaminated by the other. This is, as such, the *tour de force* we need to grasp: the "oneself" is to be made to move, to be destabilized, so that it no longer rests in peace, as Levinas puts it, "under its identity." And yet what could be more ontologically and psychologically stable than the oneself in its identity? The oneself about which Levinas is speaking is, however, an atomic, whirlwind-like oneself, a molecular quasi-multiplicity similar to that of Deleuze-Guattari, albeit marked as One: "The for-itself is a torsion irreducible to the beating of self-consciousness [. . .]. [A] presynthetic, pre-logical and in a certain sense *atomic* [. . .] unity of the self, which prevents it from splitting, separating itself from itself so as to contemplate or express itself [. . .]. It is *in a certain sense* atomic, for it is without any rest in itself, 'more and more one,' to the point of breakup, fission, openness. [. . .] It is as though the atomic unity of the subject were exposed outside by breathing, by divesting its ultimate substance even to the mucous membrane of the lungs, continually splitting up" (*OB*, 107; my emphasis).

It is not, as is sometimes said, that "thought and the prose through which it is expressed [in *Otherwise than Being*] are profoundly united"—as though Levinas had found the precise language he needed in order to "express" his thought— but rather that the exploration of otherwise than being is an exploration of the being *of* language, being *in* language. Levinas sets down repeatedly that the Saying ("antecedent to the verbal signs it conjugates," "the very signifyingness of the signification" [*OB*, 5]) is, in the linguistic system as in ontology, subordinate to the said. It is thus petrified, conceptualized, coagulated—just as is the risk of identity, which constantly threatens to arise again "like a curd coagulating for itself, [. . .] coincid[ing] with itself" (*OB*, 50). It is to this that Levinas alludes when he writes at the start of his book that "the *otherwise than being* is stated in a saying that must also be unsaid in order to thus extract the *otherwise than being* from the said in which it already comes to signify but a *being otherwise*" (*OB*, 7). The sinking of the Saying into the Said, a coagulation: this is what must be prevented. To do so, it is necessary to maintain the diachrony between *saying* [*dire*] and *unsaying* [*se dédire*], the ebb and flow of one to the other; this motion of sailing on the high seas is entailed by the extravagance of a discourse that never rests, that destabilizes being as much as it upsets language. Levinas says as much when he writes: "To conceive the *otherwise than being* requires, perhaps, as much audacity as skepticism shows, when it does not hesitate to affirm the impossibility of statement while venturing to realize this impossibility by the very statement of this impossibility" (*OB*, 7).

An Animated Language

Artaud tried to find "animated words" in language, syllables of living breath. In *Thomas the Obscure*, Blanchot imagines words as living matter, swarming and menacing: "[. . .] he perceived all the strangeness there was in being observed by a word as if by a living being, and not simply by one word, but by all the words that were in that word, by all those that went with it and in turn contained other words, like a procession of angels opening out into the infinite to the very eye of the absolute."[21] And suddenly Thomas is bitten by a word as though by a rat.[22] Levinas, too, looked to develop what he called "non-positive concepts," which is to say fluid or animated concepts, moved by a respiration that no longer allows them to rest in a tranquilly posited thesis. Just as there is no identity of the subject but "a hither side of identity" (*OB*, 114), there is no self-identity of the word, nor, *a fortiori,* of the concept. Language is thus living, not in the sense of any animist belief but in the sense of being haunted, just like the subject, by the Other that language is to itself—by being possessed, that is, by its Other, between alteration and animation, inspiration and movement, "going from said to unsaid." "Through this alteration the soul animates the subject; it is the very pneuma of the psyche. The psyche signifies the claiming of the same by the other, or inspiration, beyond the logic of the *same* and the *other,* of their insurmountable adversity" (*OB,* 141; translation modified. It is Levinas's emphasis). It is just the same in language. The soul (*animus*) animates. It is breath, air (*anima, pneumâ, psyché*). And it is with this respiration-inspiration that Levinas animates language and prevents it from coagulating; like Blanchot, he makes of it an exposition (the opposite of a position), an exile, an infinite nomadism. As Blanchot puts it in *The Infinite Conversation*: "The exigency of uprooting; the affirmation of nomadic truth."[23]

I would now like to consider two examples of this "animation" in Levinas's language (which, as he often underlined, is *absolutely not* a metaphor); this alteration (the other in the same) being that which is language's "seed of folly"—as it is the psyche's—in that it destabilizes all theses and prohibits the Saying from falling into the Said. This follows, moreover, from the fact that, for Levinas, "philosophy is perhaps but this exaltation of language in which the words, after the event, find for themselves a condition in which religions, sciences, and technologies owe their equilibrium of meaning" (*OB,* 181). I could have chosen to pursue the echoes that make rhyme and reverberate the words "obsession," "excess," "excessive," and "excession" in *Otherwise than Being,*[24] just as I could have chosen to recall the manner Levinas's philosophical discourse relies here and there on paranomasiac association (e.g., "a subjectivity that suffers [*souffre*] and offers itself [*s'offre*] before taking a foothold in being" [*OB*, 180]), or even to consider all those words that he himself called his "barbarisms"—that is to say, his way of animating, of reanimating, of making language breathe. "How can such a research be undertaken," he writes in *Otherwise than Being*, "without introducing some barbarisms in the language of [a] philosophy [. . . which] mainly remained at home in saying being, that is, inwardness to being, the being at home with oneself, of which European history itself has been the conquest and jealous defense" (*OB*, 178).

As indicated, however, I prefer to restrict myself to the following two examples:

First, the echo whose rhythm is impressed even into Levinas's reflection on being and "otherwise than being": that of the Latin *esse* (being, or essence), a word that detaches or tears itself from the stability that it was in order to become a particle (suffix) or atom of language and enter into the composition (or decomposition) of terms that it opens and alters; such that the words then decline themselves, reply to each other in echo, in a sort of exaltation of speech in which the thesis is endlessly disrupted, or destabilized ("disturbed," as Levinas would say). Hence this, for example: "The limit of the stripping bare, in the punctual core, has to continue to be torn from itself. The one assigned has to open to the point of separating itself from its own inwardness, adhering to *esse*; it must be dis-interested [*se dé-sintér*esse]" (*OB*, 49; my emphasis). And this: "The psyche is the form of a peculiar dephasing, a *loosening up* [*desserrage*] or *unclamping* [*desserre*] of identity: the same prevented from coinciding with itself, at odds, torn up from its rest, between sleep and insomnia, panting, shivering" (*OB*, 68; my emphasis). Yet another example can be found here: "The recurrence of the oneself is not *relaxed* [*ne se désserre pas*] and *tightened up* [*resserrer*] again, illuminating itself . . ." (*OB*, 104 [translation modified]; my emphasis). Indeed, we could go on ad infinitum citing examples of these sorts of drifting variants of *esse*; we are no doubt meant, moreover, to hear *esse*'s incessant echo, its almost continuous undertone, in *caresse* [caress], *tendresse* [tenderness], *mollesse* [softness], and even in *blessure* [wound]—those words that form a leitmotif throughout *Otherwise than Being.*

The second and last example, and it is a truly Artaudian and Blanchotian one, is the echo between *accusation* [accusation] and *accusatif* [accusative], another of *Otherwise than Being*'s leitmotifs. Language is again set in motion; its declension [*elle se décline*] occurs both in the looser sense and in the sense of Greek atomism: "The uniqueness of the self is the very fact of bearing the fault of another. In responsibility for another subjectivity is only this unlimited passivity of an *accusative* which does not issue out of a *declension* it would have undergone starting with the nominative. This *accusation* can be reduced to the passivity of the self only as a persecution, but a persecution that turns into an expiation" (*OB*, 112; my emphasis).[25] A little further down comes this: "To this command continually put forth only a 'here I am' (*me voici*) can answer, where the pronoun 'I' is in the *accusative, declined* before any *declension,* possessed by the other, sick, identical. [. . .] The identity of the subject is here brought out [*s'accuse*], not by a rest on itself, but by a restlessness that drives me outside of the nucleus of my substantiality" (*OB*, 142; my emphasis).

It should be noted that the "declining" of identity—in Levinas's work as much as in Beckett's *Molloy*[26]—is to be understood in all the senses of the word. While it is true that "accusative" and "accusation" have entirely different etymologies—"accusative" coming from *casus* and "accuse" from *causa,* to blame or implicate—as Levinas was obviously aware, it nevertheless remains that both words resonate here in a distorted and declined echo, in the rhythm of a signifyingness[27] that allows there to emerge and to *be*—otherwise than being—the transformation of "I" [*je*] into "here I am" [*me voici*], that is, into the accusative. The result is the breaking up of self-identity into disidentity, its being constrained thereby to an identity in which I am no longer alone, identical to myself (the "curd" in which identity constantly risks being re-coagulated) but no doubt already other than me: "The psyche, a uniqueness outside of concepts, is a seed of folly, already a psychosis. It is not an ego, but me under assignation. There is an assignation to an identity for the response of responsibility, where one cannot have oneself be replaced without fault" (*OB,* 142). It is, then, the experience of a psychosis in which the Levinassian subject comes within reach of the terrifying, paranoid invasion described by Antonin Artaud: "You think you're alone, but you're not, you're a multitude, you think you're your body, but it's something other, you think you're master of your own body, but no, it belongs to others, to another, to the other, that other that was Plato's tarantula . . ."[28] The Levinassian subject does not overlook this paranoia; he or she verges on it, examines it, fully aware. The trauma of persecution, exposure to wounding, possession of the self by the other: these are its most obvious symptoms. This experience of paranoia (a distressing experience, but one in which the subject is always fluid) is at the very heart of the experience of ethical responsibility; for alienation is indeed to be understood as necessary exposure to the other, the breakup of interiority: it is an essential "malady of identity," an accepted, or invited, madness. "Without this folly at the confines of reason, the *one* would take hold of itself, and, in the heart of its passion, recommence *essence*" (*OB,* 50; original emphasis).

Emmanuel Levinas's "seed of folly," then: it is at once the exploration of the limits of being *and* atomic particles, the multiple splinters of a shattered subjective interiority. If all psyche is psychosis, in the sense in which Levinas understands it, it is because in ecstasy—the outside-of-oneself that he imagines—we are no longer alone; the other forces its way in, extracting us from our supposed interiority, "chasing" us outside of ourselves. Thus, the caress of love "overflows with exorbitance" (*OB,* 184). This is the meaning of the "tearing-from-oneself-for-another" in *Otherwise than Being,* and we could list to our heart's content all of the expressions he coined (those necessary "barbarisms" in the language of philosophy) to signify being's exit from its dwelling place [*chez soi*]: *dé-claustration du soi-même* [opening-up of the oneself], *dé-nucléation de sa substantialité* [coring out of one's substantiality], *fission du Moi* [fission of the ego]. And so the nucleus of being explodes into a whirlwind of atoms, an infinite declension: "Here the human is brought out by transcendence, or the hyperbole, that is, the disinterestedness of essence, a hyperbole in which it breaks up and *falls upward,* into the human" (*OB,* 184; original emphasis).

Declension . . . except, for Levinas, the atoms fall *upward.*

"THERE IS NO SUCH THING AS METALANGUAGE"

Lacan and Beckett

Is it Possible to Exit Language?

I have always found Lacan's oft-repeated declaration, "There is no such thing as metalanguage," both enigmatic and deeply unsettling; there is something of Hölderlin's "we are a sign without interpretation" about it. Moreover, it is a notoriously difficult sentence to comprehend, especially given the potential confusion occasioned by Lacan's using the term "metalanguage" in a way that bears but a passing resemblance to the narrow sense accorded to it by linguists. The lecture known as "Science and Truth" (1965) leaves little doubt in this regard: "To lend my voice to support these intolerable words, 'I, truth, speak . . . ,' goes beyond allegory. Which quite simply means everything that can be said of truth, of the only truth—namely that there is no such thing as a metalanguage (an assertion made so as to situate all of logical positivism), no language being able to say the truth about truth, since truth is grounded in the fact that truth speaks, and that it has no other means by which to become grounded."[1] It goes without saying that I am not going to answer the question here of whether there is or is not such a thing as metalanguage; nor, indeed, is this the question I wish to raise. Instead, I shall try to indirectly consider this through another question, one that seems to me crucial in the domain of literary studies or literary theory, and no doubt reaching far beyond. It is a question that, for me, is formulated as follows: in what language does theory speak?

We already know Roland Barthes's answer to this question: to suggest there is such a thing as "a neutral state of language" is—he was to set down—an illusion, a "theological image imposed by science." One must, he emphasized, go beyond the opposition of language-objects and their metalanguages, an opposition that remains ultimately subject to a "paternal model of science without language."[2] We shall not discuss here whether or not this model is indeed "paternal" in character; nor shall we examine the "paternal terror" Barthes sees at work in the injunction of scientific truth that would have been imposed on the theory of the text. This was, as we know—and as he, too, knew—the fantasy of a time. The impossibility of metalanguage—of the discourse of a language emanating *from itself* to talk *about itself*—is absolute, as Derrida often said: we are forever caught in the webs that we weave, or again, in the words of that renowned formula, "There is nothing outside the text."

The Lacanian proposition that "there is no such thing as metalanguage" can, as I see it, be understood in at least two different ways. Either as an *interdiction*—indeed, as an *interdiction to think,* which is to say an utterance with an underlying threat: "Don't you dare even think that there is such a thing as metalanguage! There is not." Move along, there is nothing to see here, nothing to think. Or one might understand it in a way that is less certain, and more worrying, too. It is this second interpretation that I would like to expand upon. For it seems to me that nothing is more assertive than this particular type of negation: *there is no*

such thing as . . . And one can, of course, identify in Lacan's work an entire paradigm of *that which there is no such
thing as*: there is no such thing as metalanguage, no such
thing as the sexual relation, no such thing as the Other of
the Other, no such thing as truth about truth, etc. The sentence is, then, seemingly meant to be understood as the
assertion of a negation, and is susceptible as such to irritate
certain readers, as it did Vincent Descombes: "There is no
such thing as metalanguage, says Lacan. Perhaps so. But
how do we know?"[3] In other words, what does *he* know?
Let him prove it if he can; but how can he when he maintains that there is no such thing as metalanguage? Or must
we, on the contrary, accept it without further discussion as
an unthinkable limit, in the sense Roland Barthes gave it
in his inaugural lecture at the Collège de France: "human
language has no exterior: there is no exit"?[4]

Another hypothesis I would also like to examine is that
of understanding this sentence as a *denial* [*dénégation*].
Naturally, we must first define what we mean by "denial"
in this context. I shall therefore immediately say what, for
me, it *is not.* It is not the coercive instrument that certain
psychoanalysts make of it, confusing analysis with who-
knows-what police practice of extorting confessions, along
the lines of: if you deny it, I must be right in saying that you
admit it. When acting in this way, psychoanalysis numbers
among what Barthes calls "ideospheres," those powerful
linguistic systems that set themselves up as the total space
of language, within which, willingly or by force, you find
yourself situated, or rather incarcerated; they are coercive
systems, then, with no external lever by which to free yourself. Take this declaration from the Catholic ideosphere, for
example, which Barthes often cited: "You would not seek
me if you had not already found me." Indeed, how is one to
escape this?

On Denial/Denegation

Freud is certainly no stranger to this fiercely unilateral interpretation of denial. Remember the example he gives at the start of his famous article of 1925 entitled *Die Verneinung* (translated into English as *Negation* but which could equally be translated—into English as into French—as *"denegation,"* since both these terms are covered by the German word, which is, moreover, Freud's point), which is as follows: a patient of his says to him, "You ask who this person in the dream can be. It's *not* my mother." Freud notes, "We emend this to: 'So it *is* his mother.'" A little further on in the same article, he adds: "There is a very convenient method by which we can sometimes obtain a piece of information we want about unconscious repressed material. 'What,' we ask, 'would you consider the most unlikely imaginable thing in that situation? What do you think was furthest from your mind at that time?' If the patient *falls into the trap* and says what he thinks is most incredible, he almost always makes the right *admission.*"[5]

Nor is Lacan himself a complete stranger to this tendency psychoanalysis sometimes shows of "getting it right" by relying on the circularity of arguments that presuppose themselves. Consider that sentence-long diagnosis revered by certain of Lacan's students as one of his discoveries: My dear lady, you said "*galopiner*" . . . You must be paranoid. Denial, however, as we know, is far more than the simple reversal of no and yes, and this is precisely what Freud tried to demonstrate in his 1925 article. I am referring here, of course, to Jean Hyppolite's commentary on this work— written at Lacan's request—that highlights the complexity of the denegative structure, showing this to testify to the originary intertwining of yes and no in thought. Hyppolite reads Freud's text, moreover, as a genuine Freudian myth concerning the creation of the symbol and the genesis of thought. Lacan himself, on several occasions, emphasizes the extraordinarily fluid nature of the denegative process as envisaged by Freud, its untenable character, what it owes to expulsion and death, and even the proximity it reveals once again between Freud's thought and the pre-Socratic doctrines in the paradoxical way in which "what is simultaneously actualized and denied comes to be avowed."[6] A little further on, Lacan adds the following on denial: "One should continue this study of *Verneinung* that I have just begun with a study of the negative particle."[7] In so doing, he raises the complex question of the use of what we call the "expletive '*ne*'" in the French language.

How to Deny

What follows both is and is not an aside. In January 2001, Jacques Derrida gave a series of lectures on the "Typewriter Ribbon" at the French National Library. In the third of these lectures, the only one I was able to attend, he spoke of an error in the translation of a sentence from Rousseau's *Confessions* made by Paul de Man in his work *Allegories of Reading*. Rousseau's sentence, from Book II, reads as follows: "Mais je ne remplirai pas le but de ce livre si je n'exposais en même temps mes dispositions intérieures, et *que je craignisse de m'excuser* en ce qui est conforme à la vérité."

De Man first cites this sentence in French and adds, of his own accord, an expletive *ne* ("et que je *ne* craignisse de m'excuser . . ."). He then makes a second slightly peculiar manipulation, translating it into English with a negation proper: "and if I did not fear to excuse myself . . ." I am not going to comment, in my turn, on Jacques Derrida's commentary; rather I shall simply pick up what he says on the "expletive *ne.*" Ultimately, for him, Paul de Man's first error (the first "manipulation") is not particularly serious, as it does not in fact change anything; this, he says, is because this type of *ne* serves no purpose in the French language: "An expletive *ne* in French is a pleonastic *ne.* One may either inscribe it or not in a sentence as one wishes. [. . .] I can say '*il craint que je sois trop jeune*' or, just as well and with the same meaning, '*il craint que je ne sois trop jeune.*' These two sentences are strictly equivalent in French."[8] After the lecture, I wrote him a note essentially stating that what he had said about the expletive *ne* had perhaps been a little . . . rapid, that there were after all a number of grammarians who had reflected on this complex issue at length: I reeled off Damourette and Pichon on the discordantial, the forclusive and the "expletive," and, of course, Lacan (what he says on the expletive *ne* in Seminar VII and in *Écrits,* in the chapter entitled "The Subversion of the Subject and the Dialectic of Desire"). "You are right," he replied, "I will add a note." And indeed, when the book appeared, entitled *Paper Machine,* there was a note.[9] Derrida mentions the passages from Lacan, and in particular the one in Seminar VII in which Lacan precisely attends to the difference between "*je crains qu'il vienne*" and "*je crains qu'il* ne *vienne.*" One must not forget that, for Lacan, the *ne* is in no way pleonastic, since it designates the trace that is apparent in the signifier of the subject of the utterance. In his note, Derrida wrote the following: "One must pay attention in this passage to the strange grammar and the unstable status of the italicised *ne*: [he then cites Lacan's sentence] 'The negative particle *ne* only emerges at the moment when I really speak, and not at the moment when I am spoken, if I am on the level of the unconscious.'"[10] The note ends here without further comment. I would add just two points, the first of which is this: unlike Derrida, I did not notice the unstable *ne.* Secondly, that playing in such a way with negation and denial (but *who* is playing?—this is what is crucial) by definition risks misunderstanding. Don't say you weren't warned . . . Lacan would sometimes add.

Whether the *ne* in Lacan's sentence is expletive or restrictive does not, in my opinion, change the question. When one writes "*la particule* ne */ vient au jour qu'à partir du moment où je parle vraiment,*" it is clear that a *ne* is missing (or not missing) and that what is demonstrated here by the instability of the *ne* is the instability of all processes of denial or negation. And this is precisely what Lacan is saying here: he is speaking of the indeterminacy of a knowledge that only reveals itself to that which he calls the *mistaking* [*méprise*] of the subject. The question is whether this missing *ne* is a genuine or a fake mistaking, a purposeful misdirection. I shall return to this later.

For I now want to take a moment to consider Lacan's 1967 article "The Mistaking of the Subject Supposed to Know," first published (in French) in *Scilicet* and since reproduced in *Autres Écrits.* In it, Lacan precisely analyzes the paradoxical, aporetic, structure that underpins the act of analysis. He points out, for example, that what links analytical discourse and practice is that something can be said there "without any subject knowing it [*sans qu'aucun sujet le sache*],"[11] which is also the definition of unconscious speech. Rather than discuss in detail this "*sans qu'aucun sujet le sache* [without any subject knowing it]," I would merely point out that the aporia or non-place between yes and no, between affirmation and negation, is precisely displayed in this clause in the vacillation affecting the indefinite *aucun* [any], which oscillates between its positive value, "someone," and its negative value, "nothing, no one, not one." Indeed, it is important to remember that *aucun* is still used literarily without *ne* in the positive sense of "somebody," in accordance with its etymology (from *aliquis*, someone). When, for example, Madame de Sévigné writes to her daughter, "*Je serais bien fâchée, ma bonne, qu'aucun courrier fût noyé,*" she clearly did not mean that she wished the messenger in question to disappear without a trace.[12] *Sans qu'aucun sujet le sache* is, then, the undecidability of negation in the oscillation from yes to no, from positive to negative; it is "this aspect of the unconscious" that, Lacan writes, "does not open so long as it does not follow that it closes." *Sans qu'aucun le sache* is, then, both at once and in equal measure, "*sans que personne ne le sache* [without no one knowing it]" and "*sans que quelqu'un le sache* [without someone knowing it]." It is, in my opinion, this structure that Lacan calls indetermination; this being equally that which defines the oscillation of negation between life and death, and even, more precisely, "the order of indetermination constituted by the relation of the subject to a knowledge passing beyond it."

Maîtrise, Méprise

And the theoretical discourse of the psychoanalyst in all of this, the discourse that is certainly not a metalanguage, that hinges on the very practice of the unconscious: what language is spoken in this instance? The article I have been citing, "The Mistaking of the Subject Supposed to Know," actually starts with a fairly amusing use of negation (in the sense of a reversal of logic). Lacan writes: "All the same, it is not from the discourse *of* the unconscious that we are going to glean the theory that accounts for it." And he adds a little further on: "the discourse *on* the unconscious [is] a condemned discourse: it is only in fact sustained by the post without hope of any metalanguage."[13] On this opposition between "discourse *of* the unconscious" and "discourse *on* the unconscious," I refer to Soshana Felman's excellent commentary published in the issue of *L'Arc* dedicated to Lacan:[14] in it, she analyzes the undecidable that characterizes Lacan's speech, pulled between metalanguage (a grammar) and rhetoric (of the unconscious).

It is, however, another aspect of Lacanian rhetoric that

holds my attention here. In the same article on mistaking, Lacan opposes two subjects: on the one hand the subject of the conscious *maîtrise* [command] of speech, the subject who believes they know what they are saying and whom Lacan calls "the subject supposed to know" and, on the other hand, the subject of the *méprise* [mistaking], the subject who is mistaken, who takes one word for another, one letter for another. From *maîtrise* to *méprise,* with just one letter's, or rather one phoneme's, difference,[15] it is the same subject, and this is the entire problem precisely because the psychoanalyst has to be one and the other (or neither one nor the other). Indeed, knowledge, says Lacan, "is only delivered to the mistaking of the subject." He therefore writes the following: "In the structure of the mistaking of the subject supposed to know, the psychoanalyst (*but who is, and where is, and when is*—run the gamut of categories, which is to say the indetermination of his subject—the *psychoanalyst*?), the psychoanalyst however must find the certitude of his act and the gap that makes its law."[16]

This indeterminate subject, the subject that experiences this "atopia," is, then, the psychoanalyst caught between theory and practice, discourse and method (and not "discourse of the method": it is here, *between* discourse and method, that the gap now opens). In order to circumvent the old complicity between theory and theology, there must, says Lacan, be a lack, a breach: this is the mistaking, the hole, the slip; it is this that creates the indissociable coexistence of the interpretable and the uninterpretable. It is precisely this open, parenthetic gap that intrigues me here, and the strange, unfinished list: "but who is, and where is, and when is [. . .] the psychoanalyst?" I may be mistaken (although I do not believe I am) but I cannot help but hear in this an echo of the well-known opening to Beckett's *The Unnamable,* those first few lines that raise the very same questions ("Who I? Where I? When I?"):

Where now? Who now? When now? Unquestioning.
I, say I. Unbelieving. Questions, hypotheses, call them
that. Keep going, going on, call that going, call that on.
[. . .] Perhaps that is how it began. [. . .] What am I to
do, what shall I do, what should I do, in my situation,
how proceed? By aporia pure and simple? Or by affirmations and negations invalidated as uttered, or sooner or
later? [. . .] I should mention before going any further,
any further on, that I say aporia without knowing what it
means. Can one be ephectic otherwise than unawares? I
don't know. With the yesses and noes it is different, they
will come back to me as I go along [. . .].[17]

Beckett and Lacan

It seems to me—and it is a hypothesis I take seriously—
that Lacan's *indeterminate* subject and Beckett's *unnamable* subject are not so dissimilar from one another; one
might even say they are profoundly and secretly related, as
though, beyond their theoretical and literary differences,
one same uncertain subject (between *certainty* [*certitude*]
and *gaping* [*béance*], as Lacan says) were attempting to create existence for itself in the provisory form of a language,
its own not its own. This subject, which Beckett calls "ephectic," is a subject without certainty, an unstable subject
(something like "I am . . . perhaps"): it is not, therefore, the
rational, Cartesian subject of sensible certainty and affirmation of its existence; which is to say, not an *effective* subject
(again, just a few letters off), but rather a subject at once
both weak and all-powerful, silent and loquacious. I should
point out here, again tangentially, that not being very sure
of one's existence (as would be the modern fact) in no way
prohibits one from clinging to it vigorously, and even with
faith. This is the unusual and arresting proposition made
by Deleuze: Do we no longer believe in the world? Are we

all ephectic subjects? Well then, we must return to faith. Whether this be in cinema (as it was for Deleuze) or literature makes no difference to the proposition: what makes me believe in my life is the astounding power of conviction wielded by all fiction.

> The modern fact is that we no longer believe in this
> world. We do not even believe in the events which
> happen to us, love, death, as if they only half concerned
> us. [. . .] The link between man and the world is broken.
> Henceforth, this link must become an object of belief:
> it is the impossible which can only be restored within
> a faith. [. . .] Restoring our belief in the world—this is
> the power of modern cinema (when it stops being bad).
> Whether we are Christians or atheists, in our universal
> schizophrenia, *we need reasons to believe in this world.* It
> is a whole transformation of belief. It was already a great
> turning-point in philosophy, from Pascal to Nietzsche: to
> replace the model of knowledge with belief.[18]

And again we are reminded of Beckett: "If I go on long enough calling that my life I'll end up by believing it. It's the principle of advertising."[19] All of which then, he suggests, could have begun in this way: Freud and Lacan's myth of the origin of thought, and Beckett's myth of the origin of speech—of that which, precisely, is without origin. We must, I believe, look closer at what is similar between these two utterances—Beckett's and Lacan's—both of which are at once hollowed-out and profuse. I shall list just a few points here:

The first similarity lies in that which links the discourse of mistaking and denegation (the inextricable link this forges between being and nothingness, life and death: mistaking "promotes a nothing affirmed," writes Lacan) and the numerous figures of failure, effacement, and withdrawal in Beckett's work.

The second is in the promotion, undertaken by Lacan and Beckett alike, of the figure of *misunderstanding.* "I only expect those I speak to here *to confirm the misunderstanding,*" writes Lacan. "To confirm the misunderstanding": any reader of Beckett will recognize this as a familiar phrase. In substance, what Lacan is saying is that his speech is "not to be read" (this is the definition he gives of literature) but to be misheard/misunderstood. To be ill seen, ill said, as Beckett puts it. Of course, when it comes to misunderstanding, Lacan was well heeded, as we know. Success in failure, as Beckett would have said—or indeed the opposite! The lapsus, the misunderstanding, Lacan reminds us, is that which is never so successful as when it is overlooked [*manqué*]. The opposite, however, is not necessarily true: "Which is to say that it does not suffice that [the act] founder [*échoue*] for it to succeed, that the failure [*ratage*] alone does not open the dimension of the mistaking here in question."[20]

Finally, I believe there is a clear parallel to consider between *the absence of metalanguage* (in theory) and *the absence of work* [*oeuvre*] (in literary writing). And yet, rather than an absence of work—the expression employed by Blanchot and Foucault—it seems to me that, when dealing with literary *oeuvres-limites,* such as those of Beckett, Artaud, Blanchot, and certain others, we ought to talk about *denegation of the work*: not the stability of an absence, the stasis of a lacking or a void, but rather the *movement* that bores absence into presence, success into failure. That is to say, all in all, the infinitely plastic structure of denegation such as Lacan's discourse mobilizes it, its opening onto the abyss, the "catastrophe of thought," as Blanchot says, and its chance too. Or even, as Lacan writes so exquisitely in *Écrits,* "I can come into being by disappearing from my statement [*dit*]."[21]

"I, truth, speak . . ."

We would not be so cruel as to compare the poetic and theoretical force (inseparably linked one to the other) of Lacan's denegative writing, its power of "illegibility" [*illecture*] as he puts it, and its force of revelation, to the clumsy, stilted, and stumbling ponderousness of those theoretical discourses that—during the same period of the 1960s and '70s—barricaded themselves in their critical, linguistic, and semiotic metalanguage, in which they believed and still do, and that continue to articulate the affirmation of what they believe to be the truth about the truth.[22] Let us not make comparisons but simply read the final lines of Lacan's article on mistaking—and this is by no means a conclusion: "Retain at least this that is testified to in the text I have tossed out for your consideration [*jeté à votre adresse*]: it is that my *undertaking* [*enterprise*] does not pass beyond the act where it is a *taking* [*prise*], and that therefore this act has no chance except from its *mistaking* [*méprise*]. [And he adds further on]: The false mistaking, these two terms knotted in the title of a comedy of Marivaux, finds here a renewed sense that implies no truth of discovery."[23]

The "false mistaking," according to Lacan, is then the title of a play by Marivaux. However, as we know, Marivaux never wrote a play by this title [*La Fausse Méprise*]. He wrote, among others, *La Fausse Suivante* and *Les Fausses Confidences,* and he also wrote a play called *La Méprise* (*méprise,* full stop). Lacan's *Fausse Méprise* is, then, a genuine mistaking (since it is not a real play). And yet, one has the distinct impression that it is a "false mistaking" (a dummy error, the acting out of a Freudian slip) . . . Unless, of course, it was a real slip (a genuine mistaking?) . . . And so it goes on ad infinitum in the undecidability between yes and no, true and false, language and metalanguage.

| | | | |

We ought to note here that already in "The Freudian Thing," a lecture given by Lacan in 1955, there was the slightest of hints at this inescapable game of true or false that undermines any statement of truth. It is in these pages that we find that famous prosopopoeia of truth affirming: "I, truth, speak." And what does truth say? This, among other things: "Whether you flee me in deceit or think you can catch me in error, I will catch up with you *in the mistake* [*dans la méprise*] from which you cannot hide. Where *the most cunning* [*la plus caute*] speech reveals a slight stumbling, it doesn't live up to its perfidy—I am now publicly announcing the fact—and it will be a bit *harder* [*plus coton*] after this to act as if nothing is happening, whether in good company or bad."[24] Here, already, the mistake expresses itself (is written) in the acting out of a stumbling of language (a lapsus) that involves the evocation of a "*caute*" utterance, the cotton of which it spins so as to cut short, as though by clumsiness, the *cautèle* or *cauteleux* [cunning] it presaged—in other words, this ruse of language that, here, seemingly does the opposite of what it says.[25] And yet, with just one word, it deceives, is deceived, and speaks the truth. Clearly, then, we must consider with greater cunning, or even simply with greater caution, this Lacanian *doctrine* of truth that Derrida addresses in *The Post Card.* For it is not certain that one can reduce it so simply to a structure of veiling-unveiling or one of confidence in full speech, as Derrida postulates. Above all, and as we have seen, it is not certain that the letter is, for Lacan, merely a mouthpiece, centered on the voice—phonocentric or, indeed, phallogocentric, to use Derrida's terms.[26]

We must understand reading, says Mallarmé, "as a desperate practice." The misreading of Lacan is just as desperate a practice, but gratifying. In "The Freudian Thing," he writes this: "Psychoanalysis is the science of the mirages that arise within this field [that of the four walls that delimit the analytical space]. A unique experience, a rather abject one at that, but one that cannot be too highly recommended to those who wish to get to the crux of mankind's forms of madness, for, while revealing itself to be akin to a whole range of alienations, it sheds light on them."[27] No doubt it is this that certain lovers of metalanguage continue to deny and that Lacan, for his part, knew and did not attempt to escape, exploring, on the contrary, the common space between psychoanalysis and literature—which is to say, psychoanalysis's relationship with madness, death, the exhaustion of everything . . . as well as the cheerful lucidity it draws from this.

WHAT IS AN ARCHIVE?

Beckett, Foucault

How to Begin

Since we must begin, let us do so by discussing Michel Foucault. To my knowledge, there are at least three allusions made to Beckett in Foucault's work,[1] one of which is extremely well known: it appears in the first pages of "The Order of Discourse," the inaugural lecture he gave at the *Collège de France* on December 2, 1970. As one may remember, Foucault acts out, or in a certain sense theatricalizes, the start of his speech—the beginning of his discourse. He evokes the difficulty, the impossibility even, of beginning to speak in his name. "I wish I could have slipped surreptitiously into this discourse [. . .]. I should have preferred to be enveloped by speech, and carried away well beyond all possible beginnings, rather than have to begin it myself. I should have preferred to become aware that a nameless voice was already speaking long before me."[2] A little later he cites, without explicitly naming, *The Unnamable*—specifically the very last words of *The Unnamable,* its ending: "You must go on, I can't go on, you must go on; I'll go on, you must say words, as long as there are any, until they find me," etcetera.

We would be wrong, I believe, to see in Foucault's

reference to Beckett mere fascination. Foucault does not dream of talking like Beckett; he is speaking here of a discursive position, which he precisely names "the order of discourse." What exactly this is and how it concerns Beckett are the issues I would now like to examine by briefly re-scouring that space of discourse described in some of Beckett's later works, and in particular in "For to End Yet Again"—a text first published in French, in an earlier version, in 1972 under the title *Abandonné,* with illustrations by Geneviève Asse; it was then reworked and completed under the new title in 1975.

First of all, though, we must return to the very first time Foucault cites Beckett: a citation that is much less known, it seems to me, and one that is particularly troubling insofar as its utterance emerges from an untenable discursive and subjective paradox, something like the "horns of a dilemma," as Beckett would say. It is the response he wrote to a question posed by the magazine *Esprit* in 1968.[3] The question asked by *Esprit* is of little importance; the fact remains that Foucault wrote an answer of more than twenty-five pages, ending this time with a quote from Beckett's *Texts for Nothing* (again without acknowledgment). This response—which Foucault concludes, then, by borrowing Beckett's voice but without saying so—merits consideration. Foucault explains at length in this article what exactly is entailed by his research into what he calls the "archaeology of discourses." He reminds us of what he understands by the question of the *archive* (the set of rules that, at a given time, define the limits and forms of discourse) and lists the aspects that define this discursive archive: of what is it possible to speak, and what is it that has been constituted as the domain of discourse? As he repeats here, this requires, among other things, that we challenge "the idea of a sovereign subject which arrives from elsewhere to enliven the inertia of linguistic codes, and sets down in discourse the indelible trace of its freedom." It is, then, a question of challenging "the idea of a subjectivity which constitutes meanings and then transcribes them into discourse." Discourse, Foucault emphasizes, "is not what was 'meant'" (the charge of intentions); "it is not what has remained mute."[4] Here— and please forgive the length of this quotation—is the end of Foucault's text:

> I know as well as anyone how "thankless" such research can be, how irritating it is to approach discourses not by way of the gentle, silent, and intimate consciousness which expresses itself through them, but through an obscure set of anonymous rules. I know how unpleasing it must be to reveal the limits and necessities of a practice, in places where it has been customary to see the play of genius and freedom unfolding in their pure transparency. [. . .] Finally I know, considering how each person hopes and believes he put something of "himself" into his own discourse, when he takes it upon himself to speak, how intolerable it is to cut up, analyze, combine, recompose all these texts so that now the transfigured face of their author is never discernable. So many words amassed, so many marks on paper offered to numberless eyes, such zeal to preserve them beyond the gesture which articulates them, such a piety devoted to conserving and inscribing them in human memory—after all this, must nothing remain of the poor hand which traced them, of that disquiet which sought its calm in them, of that ended life which had nothing but them for its continuation? Are we to deny that discourse, in its deepest determination, is a "trace"? [. . .] Must I suppose that, in my discourse, it is not my own survival which is at stake? And that, by speaking, I do not exorcise my death, but establish it; or rather, that I suppress all interiority, and yield my utterance to an outside which is so indifferent

to my life, so neutral, that it knows no difference between my life and my death?

I can well understand those who feel this distress.
[. . .] They cannot bear—and one can understand them
a little—to be told: discourse is not life; its time is not
yours; in it you will not reconcile yourself with death;
it is quite possible that you have killed God under the
weight of all that you have said; but do not think that
you will make, from all that you are saying, a man
who will live longer than he. In each sentence that you
pronounce—and very precisely in the one that you are
busy writing at this moment, you who have been so
intent, for so many pages, on answering a question in
which you felt yourself personally concerned and who
are going to sign this text with your name—in every sentence there reigns the nameless law, the blank indifference: "What matter who is speaking; someone has said:
what matter who is speaking."[5]

What demands closer attention here is the sudden shift in
discourse at the moment where the "you" begins to refer
to him, Michel Foucault. He hears voices. He hears a voice
(His own? Not his own?) that speaks to him, that speaks
in his place or through which he speaks, undecidedly. . . .
A voice that predicts his effacement behind the "nameless law" of anonymous discourse, that says to him that
in writing he disappears, sinks deeper and is little by little (or suddenly?) engulfed by the "blank indifference" of
speech. And again, to conclude, Foucault quotes Beckett
without naming him, and without citing the work from
which the quote is taken: the third of his *Texts for Nothing*.[6]
It is through Beckett's anonymous voice that the nameless
law is pronounced: "someone has said: what matter who
is speaking"—someone, what matter who, whoever. Tangentially, I cannot help but think here of the anonymous

hero in Joyce's last work, HCE, "Here Comes Everybody," someone is coming, who speaks and melts into the infinite murmur of all languages. At once everyone and no one, all the names in the world and no name, the voice of discourse uttered as it disappears. Joyce, though, believed in resurrection through languages; Beckett perhaps not.

Michel Foucault hardly ever speaks about Samuel Beckett. Beckett does not figure among those writers he commonly quotes, such as Sade, Hölderlin, Klossowski, and Artaud, or to whom he dedicates entire texts, such as Bataille and Blanchot. For him, these writers all have in common the attempt to explore through their writing a space other than that of subjective interiority. It is this space, this "place without place," that he calls, along with Blanchot, "the thought from outside." The "thought from outside" is one of those vertiginous concepts with the help of which Foucault, like Blanchot—and Beckett, too, I would argue— tries to grasp that which belongs both to the order of the unthinkable and the unnamable. It is, Foucault says, an experience that functions inversely to the Cartesian experience leading to the irrefutable certainty of the I and its existence.[7] We know how Beckett made fun of this subject of certainty, transforming it, among other things, into the "ephectic subject" in *The Unnamable.* Contrary, then, to the "I think that I think," the "I say that I speak" is not self-referential. It disperses, indeed erases, this existence, Foucault states, and reveals nothing but an empty space. The "thought from outside" is not, therefore, that of the interiority of philosophical reflection and the positivity of knowledge. "Speech about speech leads us, by way of literature as well as perhaps by other paths, *to the outside in which the speaking subject disappears.*"[8] This, he adds, is the reason for which Western reason took so long to think the being of language and the danger it represents for the evidence of the "I am." "We are standing on the edge of an *abyss* that had long been invisible: the being of language only appears for itself with the disappearance of the subject." What emerges for Foucault is, then, an incompatibility between "the appearing of language in its being" and "consciousness of the self in its identity."[9]

Erasing Its Traces

Abyss, gap, void, disappearance, dispersion, effacement, place without place . . . : these are, in sum, the words Foucault uses in an attempt to grasp that which would have appeared in Western literature during the second half of the nineteenth century and which he calls the experience of an outside of our interiority. Consider the first lines of "For to End Yet Again":

> For to end yet again skull alone in a dark place pent
> bowed on a board to begin. Long thus to begin till the
> place fades followed by the board long after. For to end
> yet again skull alone in the dark the void no neck no face
> just the box last place of all in the dark the void. Place
> of remains where once used to gleam in the dark on and
> off used to glimmer a remain. Remains of the days of the
> light of day never light so faint as theirs so pale. Thus
> then the skull makes to glimmer again in lieu of going
> out.[10]

For me, it is not about looking for common themes between Beckett and Foucault. There have, of course, been several attempts at critical analysis in this sense, with similarities having sometimes been drawn between the "panopticon," about which Foucault writes in *Discipline and Punish,* and such and such an aspect of *How It Is, The Lost Ones,* or *Catastrophe.* It is not certain that this is in any way enlightening. In any case, this is not what interests me here. "For to End Yet Again" is a strange text. Just after the appearance of the *skull* (which is seen just as much from within as without, from above as below, a cranial cavity and a new hill of Golgatha . . .) there (re)emerges into this world, in which all refuge has turned to ruin, *the expelled* (straight out of the story of the same name from thirty years earlier) who is designated "the little body stark erect" (as in "Lessness" or "Ping"), after which then come two *white dwarfs* carrying a stretcher and who attempt to climb that same skull, which perhaps in turn rests on the pillow of that very stretcher. In short, this is a universe caught in a "bizarre loop," a Möbius Strip or an Escherian world; the Dutch artist Escher (1898–1972) being famous, of course, for his drawings of paradoxical, potentially infinite worlds in which staircases recursively loop on themselves such that it is impossible to ever get to the top or bottom of them, or in which a hand draws a hand drawing a hand, and so on—a world of infinite reversal of the outside and inside.

The "hero" of this very short story, "For to End Yet Again," is said to be "expelled": "There in the end same grey invisible to any other eye stark erect amidst his ruins the expelled" (151). We must of course ask ourselves certain questions: expelled from where? From what? Where is the interior and exterior of this story's seemingly limitless world, this place "without place?" In the story of 1945, "The Expelled," the character—who has been thrown down the stairs—first tries to orient himself, find points of reference in the world into which he has just been thrown: "first I raised my eyes *to the sky,* whence cometh our help, where there are no roads, where you wander freely, as in *a desert,* and where nothing obstructs your vision, wherever you turn your eyes, but the limits of vision itself."[11] In "For to End Yet Again," the expelled finds himself in a sort of desert without end, infinite, a desert that is a sky without paths or footprints . . . or the inverse. Beckett puts it as follows:

"Grey cloudless sky grey sand *as far as eye can see* long desert to begin" (151).

My first observation is this: we are faced here with that well-known phenomenon of intratextuality in Beckett's work—his texts are to be read in relation one to the other; they refer to each other. Which is to say that they are porous forms, inextricably linked and intertwining, without beginning or end. This is why, moreover, "For to End Yet Again" must be read in relation to those two other short texts of the same period: "Ping" (1967) and "Lessness" (1970). One has to consider the interplay between these three texts, their echoes, the traces of one in another, traces of an anonymous voice making itself heard. For Beckett, one does not write to leave a trace—*one's own* trace—somewhere, as in the idea of relics and remains that is so typical of human vanity, but rather to track the erasure of traces and of all memory, be this in the air, the sand, or nowhere: "that's romancing, more romancing, there is nothing but a voice murmuring a trace. A trace, it wants to leave a trace, yes, like air leaves among the leaves, among the grass, among the sand [. . .]."[12]

My second observation is that a rhythmic, quasi-mnemonic repetition runs through the entire text, whereby elements reoccur, are repeated in a different order—as though recalled with difficulty from the depths of forgetfulness. The skull is mentioned in the very first sentence: "skull alone in a dark place pent bowed on a board." What board? On a table? Or a coffin? No one knows. Toward the end, he writes "sepulchral skull" (but is it the same one?). Later, we see a stretcher carried by two dwarfs and on which, we are told, "a pillow marks the place of the head" (152). The skull is perhaps that of the expelled on the stretcher . . . Unless it is the skull of whosoever is imagining this entire scene: the position described ("pent bowed on a board") is reminiscent of the meditative pose we sometimes see in Beckett's work, such as in "Stirrings Still," where the character sits "at his table head on hands," or later in the same text where he "sink[s] his head as one deep in meditation."[13]

We might hypothesize that the "little body" that appears very early in the text, that of the expelled, is precisely what has been *imagined* by the skull, the *fruit* of its imagination, that which, in a certain sense, has been expelled from it. This would give us a rather ironic metaphor for the creation of the character: the expelled . . . straight from the brain of the writer, a creature brought into the world by his creator, "alone in the dark." Here, the moment of inspiration and myth of being born from the skull meet the myth of a death, since, as we know, the skull was for Beckett a symbol of Golgotha and the crucifixion. "Thus then the skull last place of all makes to glimmer again in lieu of going out [*au lieu de s'eteindre*]." The question is, what place is this? For this skull-womb of creation is a paradoxical place, at once and indistinguishably both a last place "to end," "to go out" (and therefore die), and a place to end "in lieu of going out" (these two meanings being generated by the ambiguity of the syntax insofar as "*au lieu de*" means both "in the place of" and "rather than"). Rather than go out, it is revived, it reignites ("all at once as if switched on"). With Beckett's writing, we never stop dying and being born again in an endless cycle of secular and parodic resurrection.

Scraps of Memory

In the field of Beckettian studies, another possibly infinite world, one particularly good paper is Sjef Houppermans's "Chutes sans fin dans *Pour Finir Encore*,"[14] in which the author correctly points out that "For to End Yet Again" is a sort of fantastical tale with nightmarish dwarfs lost in an apocalyptic landscape, a gray desert covered in dust. It is also, he says, a "journey to the end of the fall," that long-standing theme in Beckett's work where it is a question of the final fall of the lifeless body, the Entombment, with an allusion once again to Mallarmé's *The Tomb of Edgar Poe* ("calm block fallen down here from an unseen disaster"), dust to dust, traces of a way of the cross with no hope of resurrection. Unlike John Pilling, who sees "For to End Yet Again" as the search for a place *in* the spirit, Sjef Houppermans foregrounds Beckett's questioning of "the limits between imagination and real life, between interior scenarios and the outside world" and "a fundamental doubt regarding any final frontier the text hopes to establish."[15] Without taking anything away from this reading, which I find very convincing—the fantastical tale and way of the cross both undeniably feature in this text—I would, for my part, like to consider the work with regard to the construction (paradoxical, in ruins . . .) of a space of writing. "For to End Yet Again" is in many regards set up in the same way as *The Unnamable,* with the exception that it no longer explores that which is heard in discourse (*the voice* [*la voix*]) but that which is to be scrutinized (*sight* [*le voir*]), the indecipherable illegibility of a writing white on white: "Grey dust as far as eye can see beneath grey cloudless sky and there all at once or by degrees this whiteness to decipher. Yet to imagine if he can see it the last expelled amidst his ruins if he can ever see it and seeing believe his eyes" (152).

The space of writing, perhaps. An infinitely plastic and paradoxical space, an *experimental space,* as always in Beckett's writing. Indeed, for Beckett, as we have seen, it is a matter less of a fictional imaginary than an experimental one, an imaginary of hypothesis, assumption, and experimental protocol: we assume there is some body (some "little body") rather than nothing. Or let us pose on a board a "skull alone in the dark," which is to say, a cylinder; let us imagine "two zones form[ing] a roughly circular whole";[16] let us suppose that "a voice comes to one in the dark . . ." Here, we must remind ourselves of the structure put in place at the beginning of *The Unnamable,* with the narrator making the hypothesis of a place "which *spews me out or swallows me up* [this is the question already posed in "The Expelled," asked again in "For to End Yet Again"], I'll never know, which is perhaps merely the inside of my distant skull [note the strange expression: *a distant . . . inside*] where once I wandered, now am fixed, lost for tininess, or straining against the walls, with my head, my hands, my feet, my back, and ever murmuring my old stories, my old story, as if it were the first time."[17]

Remember that *The Unnamable* more or less starts with these words: "Yes, it is to be wished, to end would be wonderful, no matter who I am, no matter where I am." And let us once again read the start of "For to End Yet Again": "For to end yet again skull alone in a dark place pent bowed on a board to begin. [. . .] Skull last place of all black *void within without* till all at once or by degrees this leaden dawn at last checked no sooner dawned" (151; my emphasis). In the penetrating and dazzling reading Maurice Blanchot proffered of the trilogy (and which has at times been quite seriously misread), he underlines the extent to which Beckett's speech is a "wandering speech, one that is not deprived of meaning, but deprived of center."[18] Blanchot says that Molloy, for example, is caught in an important movement, a movement of wandering [*errance*] and error [*erreur*], which is "accomplished in a region that is one of *impersonal obsession.*"[19] It should be noted here how strange and intriguing is this notion—so astoundingly different in comparison to psychoanalysis—of an "impersonal obsession." We must, I believe, try to understand what Blanchot means by this, which is nothing less than a mad paradox: namely, what one finds arrayed in Beckett's work is a space describing and inscribing an *interior exteriority* or, alternatively, an *exterior interiority*: "the inside of my distant skull," as is written in *The Unnamable.* Understood as such, *The Unnamable* is not an interior monologue but rather an *exterior* monologue, if we might put it this way. Moreover, *The Unnamable* usefully says as much: to write is a "bitter folly."

What is it, then, that characterizes this mad space in "For to End Yet Again," this space of "inside outside" as Beckett puts it? I list just a few of its traits below:

First, its function as an *archive* (understood as personal and impersonal memory). There is, as we know, in Beckett's work an internal *memory* of the text, an auto-textual[20] memory in which everything tends to repeat and where everything said has already been said elsewhere, either *in* that very text (*inside* then) or *outside* it (i.e. in another of Beckett's works, or, of course, in another *other* text, *not* by Beckett). I shall not labor the point; every Beckett reader is familiar with this function of the text, the very symbol of which could be "Lessness," with its cleverly calculated repetitions. The question is, what is the memory involved? Who remembers? It is of course too simple to reply merely that it is the memory of Samuel Beckett ("I invented my memories," *The Unnamable* says moreover) or of the reader. Let us recall that throughout his text on Proust, Beckett develops this idea of memory fragments. The *Search,* in Beckett's eyes, far from being a cathedral edified against time, actually celebrates a memory in ruins, a work built on the "crumbs and fragments" of time. Beckett's memory archive is just as much in the skull as it is dispersed outside of it. It is a memory that combines, inside-outside, "all the memory of the world," as Alain Resnais would put it, on the condition that it be understood not as recollection, a collection or a library, but rather as dispersion, an infinite sowing of texts. The memory of no one. It is, then, some of these memory scraps of earlier works that *return* (in the spectral sense) in "For to End Yet Again," that we shall now take into consideration.

The first example, already met with, is the reappearance of the *expelled* as one of the returning "characters" in "For to End Yet Again." The expelled, in the story of the same name, finds himself at the bottom of some steps following a fall in the form of a birth and shares his disarray from the very outset: "I did not know where to begin nor where to end, that's the truth of the matter."[21] He returns in "For to End Yet Again" as a "little body," a corpuscle of textual matter, the debris of gray matter (he is there amongst *his* ruins, the ruins of himself); he is incorporated, if I can put it this way, within the slow erosion of matter that has over time created the infinite landscape of gray desert that surrounds him, as if the landscape, the desert, were made of his ruined body and he himself, the expelled, were the origin of the desert that surrounds him. Which is expelled from which? Impossible to say. Where is the inside and the outside? In any case, if there is a "story" at all in this account (?), it is that of the expelled's end. But naturally, it is not an end: "Last change of all in the end the expelled falls headlong down and lies back to sky full little stretch amidst his ruins. Feet centre body radius falls unbending as a statue falls faster and faster the space of a quadrant. Eagle the eye that shall discern him now mingled with the ruins mingling with the dust beneath a sky forsaken of its scavengers" (153).

The second example is the return of *The Unnamable.* There are a great many instances we could evoke to show the extent to which "For to End Yet Again" is arranged along lines similar to that of *The Unnamable* (whence the continuity, in spite of everything, of Samuel Beckett's undertaking). So, for example, the expelled describing the semi-circle of a fall (axis and radius) as much backwards as forwards, and the two dwarfs with their rotation around the

axis of the stretcher, tracing the erratic course of bodies—
(indistinctly) celestial or terrestrial—turning about the immobile skull. Just like Malone in *The Unnamable*: "it would
follow that Malone, wheeling about me as he does, would
issue from the enceinte at every revolution [. . .] he wheels
[. . .] about me, like a planet about its sun." The skull in
"For to End Yet Again" harks back to "the great smooth ball
[. . .] featureless, but for the eyes . . ." in *The Unnamable*—
that from which the nose, the hair, and the eyes have fallen
("of the fall of my ears heard nothing"). The inquiring eye
in "For to End Yet Again" is, furthermore, not without similarity to that of the Master, that taciturn being in *the Unnamable* who watches with his "livid eye."

The third and last example of these memory scraps
of other texts is that renowned recollection of a question
posed to the mother about the sky and earth. I list its occurrences briefly below, as it is important to consider them
in order of appearance:

> "The End": "Now I was making my way through the
> garden. There was that strange light which follows a
> day of persistent rain, when the sun comes out and the
> sky clears too late to be of any use. The earth makes
> a sound as of sighs and the last drops fall from the
> emptied cloudless sky. A small boy, stretching out his
> hands and looking up at the blue sky, asked his mother
> how such a thing was possible. Fuck off, she said."[22]
>
> *Malone Dies*: "One day we were walking along the road,
> up a hill of extraordinary steepness [just like the two
> dwarfs climbing up the skull], near home I imagine,
> my memory is full of steep hills, I get them confused.
> I said, The sky is *further away* than you think, is it not,
> mama? It was without malice, I was simply thinking of
> all the leagues that separated me from it. She replied,
> to me her son, It is precisely *as far away* as it appears
> to be. She was right. But at the time I was aghast."[23]

> *Company*: "Looking up at the *blue sky* and then at your
> mother's face you break the silence asking her if it is
> not in reality *much more distant* than it appears. The
> sky that is. The *blue sky.* Receiving no answer you men-
> tally reframe your question and some hundred paces
> later look up at her face again and ask her if it does not
> appear much less distant than in reality it is. For some
> reason you could never fathom this question must have
> angered her exceedingly. For she shook off your little
> hand and made you a cutting retort you have never for-
> gotten."[24]

The same episode, misplaced and distorted, features in
"Lessness": "He will curse God again as in the blessed days
face to the *open sky* the passing deluge. Face to calm eye
touch close all calm all white all gone from mind."[25] I have
chosen to leave aside the psychological aspect (the hypo-
thetical maternal rejection, the psychological wound, etc.),
as I have that of salvation (how far are we from heaven [*le
ciel*]?[26]). I have retained only the core here of this recurring
trait: namely, the question of emptiness and fullness (the
perforated sky, the deluge, the opening, infinite blue, as far
as the eye can see). The question is one of limits, then, of
near and far, belonging and wrenching away (again, what
is expelled and from what?), of that which separates the
sky from the earth, the outside from the inside, and so on.
These questions resurface in "For to End Yet Again" with
the final dream of a space at last without limits, without
coordinates, neither heaven nor earth (without trace, sign,
or writing), an infinite expanse as far as the eye can see
(without beginning or end) beneath a same gray cloudless
sky: "grey cloudless sky glutted dust verge upon verge hell
air not a breath? And dream of a way in *a space with neither
here nor there* where all the footsteps ever fell can never
fare nearer to anywhere nor from anywhere further away?"
(153; my emphasis).

All of this is like a dream of an archive in Foucault's sense, an archive in which the individual subject is erased in the anonymous space of discourse and writing. Memory is, then, no longer mine, but that of a writing becoming anonymous—something there that traces and undoes itself. The poetic rhythm of these final works *is,* moreover, an effect of this textual, trans-individual memory, in which that which is remembered returns as a form of movement, discursive fragments, shards of recollections. It is indeed as an "organization of the moving" and the "organization of subjectivity in speech" that Henri Meschonnic describes rhythm, although this holds only on condition that one does not confound individual and subject, nor—we might add—subjective memory and personal, or individual, memory. In "For to End Yet Again," one of the forms this rhythm takes consists in the suppression of agential subjects in favor of subjectless pronominal verbs, as though *it* literally created itself, wrote itself directly in the sand or the dust, as though the letters more or less traced themselves. Hence, for example, the following: "*Se remet* donc ainsi à *se faire* encore pour finir encore le crâne [. . .]. *S'y lève* enfin soudain ou peu à peu et magique *s'y maintient* un jour de plomb" (*Pour Finir Encore*).[27] In other words, the skull manifests itself (*il se fait . . . le crâne*) just as does daylight or the hour, in a totally impersonal process.[28] It is, in a way, an ultimate and diminished *fiat lux*: "Let there be light!" Let there be the skull but in a weak light, the remains of a pale day.

Cuttings and Falls

One last trait to finish on. The archive in Beckett's work has to be understood as a continually resumed and re-examined investigation of the boundaries between outside and inside (the limits of "sayability [*dicibilité*]" as Foucault says: in all discourse, there exist limits, conditions of emergence and disappearance). In this sense, the archive is also the *arkhè*, the principle of origin, the place where things begin, the place without place where they take place. I should also mention here Jacques Derrida's suggestion, in *Archive Fever*, that the archive would be the first cryptic inscription tracing the limits between inside and outside, and that which, at once both public and private, home and museum, gathers, rejects, or expels: "But where does the outside commence? This is the question of the archive. There are undoubtedly no others."[29]

As with the glossolalics, those enlightened madmen and mystics studied by Michel de Certeau who claim to "speak in tongues," there is in Beckett's work an exploration of the boundaries of speech and writing. Like them, he seeks to discover how speech is born (where it comes from, from what silence, from what absence) and how it is extinguished. As in theirs, there is in Beckett's work a play on the shift from mutism (*not being able* to say) to speech (*being able* to say) and the inverse: a shift from a *flood* of words and tears (the *not being able* to be quiet, the "I must go on") to silence ("I can't go on").

How is speech born? As we know, in Samuel Beckett's texts the way in which rhythm and scansion are ordered depends on a nonpersonal segmentation [*une découpe non personnelle*]. Beckett constantly *cuts out* [*découpe*] and searches (against an indistinguishable background of fog, of gray . . .) for how light extracts speech, how beams of light bring faces into relief [*découpent*], how syntactic, poetic, and rhythmic scansion describes (also in its plastic and figurative sense) something of the *emergence of forms.*

Where to cut [*couper*]? This is, of course, a question that all Beckett readers ask themselves constantly. Where are the breaks? Just one example from "For to End Yet Again": "Monstrous extremities including skulls stunted legs and trunks monstrous arms stunted faces." What exactly is monstrous? The extremities, including the skulls and legs but not counting the trunks? Or counting them? How does one measure the monstrousness? What is a "monstrous" dwarf?

Another question: how to begin? The answer is not by will, subjective intention, or individual initiative but by laws of physics: attraction, weight, the fall of bodies, gravity, and commutation. The "commutator," or "switch," controls here the movement between black and gray, from black to the void. Let us reread the beginning of the work: "By degrees less dark till final grey or all at once *as if switched on* grey sand as far as eye can see beneath grey cloudless sky same grey" (note in passing the difficulty of inserting a break around "as if switched on"). Or, again, the end of the text: "No for in the end for to end yet again by degrees or as though switched on dark falls there again . . ." We ought also to remember *The Lost Ones*: "The murmur cut off *as though* by *a switch* fills the cylinder again."[30]

How to go on? The whole text is, simply stated, built on *switching*, substitutions, reversals (of perspectives and roles), alternation, ebb, and flow: "In the end the feet as one lift clear the left forward backward the right and the amble resumes." And again the stretcher bearers: "They carry face to face and relay each other often so that turn about they backward lead the way." *Permutation* is yet another feature—"Swelling the sheet now fore now aft as *permutations* list a pillow marks the place of the head," (my emphasis)—this being a law of distribution of textual fragments, equivalences the text weaves: *ruins, sand, dust, fragment, desert, ashes* . . . And yet further, there is a vertical paradigm of sound: *paupières* [eyelids], *désert* [desert], *civière* [litter], *mère* [mother], *air* [air], *enfer* [hell], *chimère* [chimera], *funéraire* [sepulchral] . . .

How to end? At last. How does speaking come undone? Through a *fall*: of the little body, the refuge, the fragments of ruins, the night, and so on (I refer you here to Sjef Houppermans's text), but also through *lapsus.* Lapsus ("fallen" in Latin) is a textual variant of the fall. Certain examples of lapsus in "For to End Yet Again" intensify the fall of the bodies, their submission to the laws of weight and universal gravity. "*Ou venu d'une* lie de vie,"[31] which combines "*ligne de vie* [lifeline]" and "*lie-de-vin* [wine lees]," those dregs that form in the liquid and fall to the bottom of the container. Lees are, then, another form of fall: a double lapsus. Another example is found in "*Entre lui et elle* à vue d'oiseau *l'espace ne va pas diminuant . . . ,*" which combines "*à vue d'oeil* [visibly/before one's eyes]" with "*à vol d'oiseau* [as the crow flies]."[32] And lastly, at the very beginning of the text, "*Reste des jours du jour jamais lumière aussi faible que* la leur *aussi pâle,*" which catches the reader out, makes him or her stumble over the word (as with the false lapsus of *champagne, campagne* in *Mal Vu Mal Dit*): was that *la leur* [theirs] or *la lueur* [the light]?[33]

Lapsus, or falling, is similarly incited by the *holes* that open up in Beckett's sentences—virtually under the reader's feet, so to speak—and into which there is a literal risk of falling (like the expelled). They are blanks regularly interspersed in sentences that crumble and fall into ruin; voids that move between the words of a discourse incessantly coming apart at the very place it is put together. I am referring here not only to Beckett's use of constructions that are systematically parataxical, without any syntactic or syntagmatic links within the sentence, but more specifically to un-filled gaps. Consider this one example: "Or murmur from some dreg of life after the lifelong stand / . . . / fall fall never fear no fear of your rising again." This is a warning, perhaps addressed to the reader. And indeed, that which also function as lapsus or, in other words, as stumbling blocks over which we are invited to fall, are the changes, derivations, and displacements that mislead the reader, that cause him or her to hesitate. Hence "*le crâne* lieu *dernier* au lieu *de s'éteindre* [the skull makes to glimmer again in lieu of going out]" (9), and "*petit corps raide debout* [little body stark erect]" (instead of "*raide mort* [stone dead]"), to give but two examples.

Let us cut to the conclusion. Consider that famous quote, "If [. . .] some event of which we can at the moment do no more than sense the possibility—without knowing either what its form will be or what it promises—were to cause [these arrangements] to crumble, as the ground of Classical thought did, at the end of the eighteenth century, then one can certainly wager that man would be erased, like a face drawn in sand at the edge of the sea." These are Michel Foucault's words, the last of his book *The Order of Things.* They could just as easily be Samuel Beckett's.

AT THE LIMIT . . .

A Reading of Samuel Beckett's *That Time*

*From one end to the other of this human life which is
our lot, the consciousness of the paucity of stability,
even of the profound lack of all true stability, liberates
the enchantment of laughter.*

—Georges Bataille, *Inner Experience*

Writing against Depression

I have always found it difficult to write about Beckett's
work. Every time I do, I tell myself it will be the last. That it's
over. Never again Beckett's old stories with their old men
who never stop rambling, those gray, empty expanses as far
as the eye can see. Yet every time, including this one, I find
myself returning to it, starting to read his texts again, to
write about them. There are no doubt many reasons Beckett is such an ordeal but the primary one it seems to me
has to do with the fact that—unless we have become too
psychologically "normalized" (or rather "normopathized,"
if you will allow the expression; which is to say, barricaded
behind a strong, narcissistic armor that dulls our affect)—
we all react defensively, by way of self-preservation, when
faced with Samuel Beckett's work, and particularly his final
texts. We protect ourselves, then, by speaking of these texts'
abstraction, their mathematical precision or "prosodic

construction of being": all so many ways by which critical discourse seeks at times simply to survive.

It seems to me that, in order to read Beckett's work or to see it staged—particularly as regards the increasingly short texts he began writing at the end of the 1950s (*Krapp's Last Tape, Embers*)—we must first of all experience, or reexperience, Samuel Beckett's depression. All his life, as is known, he wrote *against* depression. His periods of creative activity were more or less brief, more or less intense, but each consisted in a hard-won, fleeting victory—not over the decomposition of bodies and words, as one might think, but over rigid forms: forms dead of meaning. I shall come back to this, but I wanted to make clear from the outset that, for me, there is no other way of reading Beckett except through joining him in this antidepressive decomposition. In my view, and contrary to what we often believe, it is when we focus too intently on forms that we become "normopathized" or slide into depression. This is the price to be paid in order that reading Beckett become amusing and exhilarating—even astonishingly beautiful. One must therefore always aim for a dynamic reading in the etymological sense of the term, that is to say a reading that makes the text shift, gives it movement, or, in other words, that rediscovers what writing is for Beckett: what he once called a "form in movement" (not a dead form).

But what is there to say here that has not already been said? First, there is the repetition of "that time again . . ." and, hence, the short play entitled *That Time*, to be understood both as "that time again" in the sense of repetition and "that time then" in the sense of a memory or days past. The text plays on this very ambiguity.

One might—so as not to read *in sequence* a text that has neither true beginning nor end—start with these two sentences taken from the very middle (but then where is the middle? "Am I right in the centre?" repeats Hamm):

"till just one of those things you kept making up to keep
the void out just another of those old tales *to keep the
void from* pouring in on top of you the shroud"

"or alone in the same the same scenes making it up
that way to keep it going *keep [the void] out* on the
stone"

"that time in the end when you tried and couldn't [. . .]
couldn't any more no words left to *keep [the void] out*"[1]

But what could it possibly mean to "keep out the void"?
At least two different things, on which language (and Beckett) plays: either the words speak in lieu of the void, they *fill* it (with "keep out" meaning here "repress" or "hold back"), or they *confine* the void within themselves, subsuming it.[2] Indistinguishably, then, and in no way contradictorily, the words are inside the void and the void is inside the words. They fill it just as it fills them. It is this paradoxical topology, *at the limit* of madness, that I want to examine in Samuel Beckett's work and particularly in his last, short, "minimalist" texts. Reversing all notion of container and contained, of outside and inside, closure and opening, they invite us to write the infinite and explore what Emmanuel Levinas called, speaking about Blanchot, a "sojourn devoid of *place*."[3]

Dusty Death

That Time is a play Beckett originally wrote in English, between June 1974 and August 1975, just after *Not I.* It is a text typical of Beckett's writing at the limit—which is primarily why I have chosen to write about it here, along with certain others. Not long before the play was performed in London, he confided to James Knowlson that he was aware of having written a play "at the very edge of what was possible in the theatre."[4] We are, indeed, no doubt at the limit of the performable.

Beckett suggested that the play was a sort of twin or little brother to *Not I,* written two years prior. *Not I* is, as we know, based on the single image of a "mouth on fire," reeling off at speed a text that is initially unintelligible—and to which listens, a little way off on the same stage, an indeterminate auditor, hooded in a djellaba. The design of these two plays (*That Time* and *Not I*) and their technical staging are so similar that Beckett made clear he did not want them to be performed together as part of the same show. "The thread is the same," he is reputed to have said. In *That Time,* the focus is on a single "character" called the Listener in English (again an auditor, just as in *Not I*) and the *Souvenant* [Rememberer] in French. The audience has what one critic called "an illuminated portrait" of the Listener. The latter's head is lit up and appears as though suspended in the darkness three meters above the stage. When the play begins, the stage is in darkness and one can hear "scraps of a single and same voice, his own," scraps called ABC and which come to him from speakers situated on both sides and above. A sonorous and musical tryptic, as some have rightly called it. That, in sum, is the set-up. It's relatively "nontheatrical" in the traditional sense of the term.

That Time is one of those Beckettian texts that I find bizarrely fascinating, almost hypnotic: it is at once very dark, despairing, and thus depressing (in the same vein as *A Piece of Monologue, Rockaby,* and *Ohio Impromptu*), yet at the same time astoundingly light, as though airborne or detached—suspended, perhaps, like the Listener's head floating above the stage. On the one hand, then, this is indeed a play dominated by darkness, loss of memory, solitude, death, and the dust that buries everything in the end. Remember the almost final words (spoken by voice C, that of the old man) declaring "not a sound only the old breath and the leaves turning and then suddenly this dust whole place suddenly full of dust when you opened your eyes from floor to ceiling nothing only dust and not a sound [. . .]" (395).

But this is not exactly how it ends. For, on the other hand, at the very end of the play the eyes of the Listener open (he has had them alternatively open or closed throughout, following the rhythm of a strange slow-motion blinking—another point to which I shall return). His eyes open; we can still hear his slow and regular breathing (another rhythm); and then—I hesitate to call it a moment of "pure theatricality," but it really is—a smile is suddenly drawn across the Listener's face, "toothless for preference." Then: "Hold 5 seconds till fade out and curtain." It certainly is a dramatic moment; in fact, it is the only event in a play in which nothing moves and, from a staging point of view, in which absolutely nothing happens (or rather nearly nothing, except for those eyes alternating between closed and open). There is not even, as in *Play,* the beam of the projector that "extracts" speech in turn from each of the three heads protruding from the urns. Nor is there anything like the frenetic movement of lips and tongue in the Mouth as it spurts out its flood of words in *Not I.* Not even the light rocking of a lullaby. Nothing.

What is this strange ending smile, then, at odds with the apparent dominance of death and dust in those last lines? It comes primarily as a gesture of nose-thumbing (insofar, at least, as a smile can be a thumbing of the nose). It is in any case a sort of incongruity, a false note come to break the uniformly tragic atmosphere of the end—a Shakespearean end, no less, if we are to believe Knowlson, who compares the dust that fills everything to the "dusty death" of Macbeth's final soliloquy. This speech takes place, let us recall, in the last act, when they have just informed Macbeth of the Queen's (Lady Macbeth's) death, prompting him to give this brief eulogy: "Tomorrow, and tomorrow, and tomorrow, creeps in this petty pace from day to day to the last syllable of recorded time, and all our yesterdays have lighted fools the way to dusty death. Out, out, brief candle!"⁵ It is just after this that he utters that famous Shakespearian line ("Life's but a walking shadow, a poor player that struts and frets his hour upon the stage and then is heard no more"). This, then, is the dusty or powdery death that little by little buries in Beckett's work the walking shadow that is the Listener and his spectral voices.

To Be Passing Through

The Listener's toothless smile is, of course, in stark contrast to the tragic atmosphere. Although reversed, this dissonance is in fact exactly the same as that at the end of *Ill Seen Ill Said*, the last pages of which evoke encroaching death, the day's end, life's end; and yet the final word is "happiness" ("Know happiness"). Let us consider this idea of dissonance for a moment, making sure not to prescribe a psychological intention to the Listener's toothless smile: it is neither mocking nor derisive nor sardonic . . . It simply *is*. Remember, too, Beckett's comments to Alan Schneider, the first director to stage *Not I*, in 1972, in response to a question about the floating and solitary image of the mouth: "'I no more know where she is or why than she does,' he wrote. There was only the text and the stage image [. . .]. 'The rest is Ibsen.'"⁶ Let us forget then Ibsen (a Joycean reference, we might note in passing) and merely remark that the toothless smile that ends the play is equivalent to *The Unnamable*'s "I'll go on": "I can't go on, I'll go on." Here, it is more "I succumb, buried in dust . . . I smile." It is the same unresolved and radical opposition; it remains there, suspended, on the edge of imbalance.

It is this suspension I want to examine here, a suspension that gives rise to a whole series of *passings* [*passages*] that bring movement to the text, or in other words that bring the text paradoxically *to life*. First, though, we need to say a word or two about the scraps of "stories" we are recounted in *That Time*. There are, as we know, three voices: A, B, and C. These are difficult to define, since Beckett's conception of the play changed as he was writing it. Initially, he had, of course, intended that the fragments of the three voices heard by the Listener embody three moments, three different stages of his earlier life—as a young man, a middle-aged man, and an old man—although not necessarily in that order, since, as we shall see, the idea of disorder and uncertainty is at the very core of the text. Memories therefore return to him in fragments and waves, seemingly in a random order although linked by a secret logic as all memories are. Beckett had intended voice A to be that of the confusion of names and places, voice B that of confusion of thought, and voice C that of confusion of feelings. Ultimately, none of this is very clearly defined in the final version, even if something of it is still discernable.

We are seemingly confronted with three parallel series of memories, which are also, as Beckett was to indicate, fragments that are at times autobiographical, memories from his own life:

1. Those spoken by voice A, revisiting childhood haunts, searching at the very top of a town that might be Dublin for the ruins of a "Folly" (no doubt in both senses of the word: psychical madness and an ornamental building or place of enjoyment). The text begins: "that time you went back that last time to look was the ruin still there where you hid as a child when was that." Leitmotif: sitting on a flat stone, surrounded by nettles and inventing stories.

2. The memories of voice C (the second to speak, the last to fall silent, with no sign of chronological order), trying alternately to invent and uninvent itself, if I can put it this way (create and "de-create" as

Beckett would say), and which "gads about" as it does so, staggering from place to place. Consider: "the rain and the old rounds trying making it up that way as you went along how it would work that way for a change never having been how never having been would work." Leitmotif: sitting on a marble slab, sheltered from the cold and rain inside a public building (museum, library, post office) and waiting to dry off (referring to clothes but also inspiration—for the mouth to "dry up," as he puts it), waiting for closing time when one would be thrown out.

3. Lastly, the memories of voice B, remembering a perhaps made-up love story that takes place in a possibly Irish countryside. Leitmotif: sitting on a stone, surrounded by indifferent nature and asking oneself if one really exists.

In each voice, then, there is immobility, solitude, and silence. The refrain they intone is: "no sign of life not a soul abroad," "no sound not a word," "no stir or sound." They are voices slowly vanishing, gathering scraps of memories before death, the void, dust, or some "great shroud" (as the text sets down) comes to bury them. These scraps and fragments would therefore all seemingly be telling the same hopeless story, mapping out a single destiny, with both beginning and end; the whole text leading, as a result, toward the inexorable extinction of these voices, their effacement, the death of the Listener. But is this really what is happening?

The Passing of Time

First, the text does, after all, form a loop; it closes in on itself as a circle. It begins with "Curtain. Stage in darkness" and ends with "[. . .] till fade out and curtain." Curtain—darkness—darkness—curtain: the series forms a chiasmus.

In other words, it is circular rather than linear, a little like *Play,* written ten years earlier, which begins over and over again; Beckett having written "Repeat" at its end. Note that he does not state whether one should ever stop repeating the play, ever stop starting everything again from the beginning upon reaching the end, and so on, ad infinitum.

Secondly, the "that time" that gives the play its title and punctuates most of the voices' interjections belongs to no specific temporality: it floats, just like the Listener's head, suspended above the stage. When was "that time," when did it begin? The voices ask themselves these very questions. For example, voice B (that which tells the love story) says: "or that time alone on your back in the sand and no vows to break the peace when was that an earlier time a later time before she came after she went or both before she came after she was gone and you back in the old scene wherever it might be might have been the same old scene before as then then as after [. . .] that time you went back soon after long after" (393).

There is a clear confusion of temporality, with neither before nor after clearly defined, with no possibility of orienting oneself chronologically—there is not the merest of fixed points to betray the start point, the moment at which it all began, then recommenced. What is a "that time" that relates to no temporality? Time, here, as always in Beckett's work, stalls ad infinitum, out of bounds.

Moreover, is "that time" definitely *one* time or rather an infinity of times that have begun again, always more or less the same? And indeed, the Listener's voice (voices) endeavor(s) in vain to orient themselves in the uninterrupted flow of all those times, all those instants, the repetition of scenes never quite the same, always the same, or nearly. Once, a glider passed over the heads of the two lovers and, ever since, that same glider has been passing over endlessly. Come to that, did it ever actually pass over?

> VOICE B: "the glider passing over / never / any change
> same blue skies nothing / ever / changed" (394).

Or again, that old Beckettian question: when did it all really *begin*? When was the first time? Is there a boundary,
a limit, a start to it all? After all, can one ever be sure of
having been born at a moment or another, were it just one
time, sometime ago?

> VOICE C, THAT OF THE OLD MAN: "the one the first and
> last that time curled up worm in slime when they lugged
> you out and wiped you off and straightened you up never
> another after that never looked back after that was that
> the time or was that another time" (390).

And inversely, at the other extreme: will we really die one
day, will it end at last, once and for all . . . really, one last
once-and-for-all, so to speak? The question is especially
relevant, since, in this work diffracted into three voices,
Samuel Beckett is, I believe, experimenting with a rather
surprising temporal paradox, one that is unsettling for the
spectator-reader. It is no longer, as in *Waiting for Godot*, a
matter of waiting for a future event that never comes, that
will never happen, but rather, by a strange contortion of
time, of waiting for a *past* event, an event one has never
stopped waiting for not to take place. The result being that
one at last knows in retrospect that, that time, nothing
happened. What one remembers, then—to put this in yet
another way—is an absence of event that has never ceased
to not happen . . .

> VOICE C: "never the same after that never quite the same
> [. . .] you *could never be the same* after crawling about
> year after year sunk in your lifelong mess muttering to
> yourself who else *you'll never be the same* after this *you
> were never the same* after that" (390; my emphasis).

"after this," "after that" . . . but *that what*? That . . . nothing! Nothing, in this quagmire where all temporal markers are confused ("could," "will," "were never . . . the same") . . . Until voice C, as always, asks: "never the same but *the same as* [*whom*]."[7] "The same as whom . . . ?": a good question indeed, since no fixed identity could ensure the referential stability of such a subject.

Particles of the Ego

The question, then, is this: is *That Time* (and indeed *Krapp's Last Tape* to a certain extent) Beckett's *In Search of Lost Time*? Let us reconsider for a moment Beckett's *Proust* (1930). According to Beckett, the hypothesis Proust set out to explore (as I interpret his reading of Proust, at least) is that the passing of time within us determines us as *passing beings* [*êtres de passage*] or, in other words, as transient and perpetually changing. The action of time results in "an unceasing modification of [. . .] personality, whose permanent reality, if any, can only be apprehended as *a retrospective hypothesis.* The individual is the seat of a constant process of decantation, decantation from the vessel containing the fluid of future time, sluggish, pale, and monochrome, to the vessel containing the fluid of past time, agitated and multicolored by the phenomena of its hours."[8] This, then, is what Beckett saw in Proust's work: there is no permanence of being. Everything flows, slides, ceaselessly passes from one state to another: we are a fragile sequence of unstable moments. This brings to mind Watt, who sometimes felt everything move and slide about him, dissolve in a swarm of sand grains:

> Gliss—iss—iss—STOP! I trust I make myself clear. There is a great alp of sand, one hundred metres high, between the pines and the ocean, and there in the warm moonless night, when no one is looking, no one listening,

in tiny packets of two or three millions the grains slip,
all together, a little slip of one or two lines maybe, and
then stop, all together, not one missing, [. . .]. It was a
slip like that I felt, that Tuesday afternoon, millions of
little things moving all together out of their old place,
into a new one nearby, and furtively, as though it were
forbidden.[9]

It is also similar to the hallucination experienced by
Malone, who describes the bizarre vision of a hand picking
out, one by one, the particles from which he is made: "I see
us again as we are, namely to be removed grain by grain
until the hand, wearied, begins to play, scooping us up and
letting us trickle back into the same place, dreamily as the
saying is. [. . .] the sensation is familiar of a blind and tired
hand delving feebly in my particles and letting them trickle
between its fingers."[10]

Let us call this, then, a Proustian experience, as revised
by Beckett, of the atomization of time, space, and bodies. I
specify "as revised by Beckett" because one naturally cannot be certain that this is exactly what Proust meant. What
interests me here, though, is precisely the interpretation,
the reading Beckett gives of Proust, insofar as it seems to
anticipate, as early as the 1930s, a conception of the real
and the subject as fundamentally atomist and decomposed. What Beckett reads in Proust's work is, then, that
we are plural and successive beings, or, in other words, that
"countless subjects [. . .] constitute the individual."[11] But
what is it that allows us, in spite of everything, to continue saying "I," to gather ourselves temporarily into a unified
subject? There are two things, according to Proust-Beckett:
habit first of all, then voluntary memory.

Voluntary memory, says Beckett, is the "emissary of
[. . .] habit" that assures, for example, the sleeper when they
awake that their ego has not disappeared along with their

tiredness, that they are still "the same" (but as the other says, "the same as whom?"). In any case, it is this memory that assures our permanence, our stability of identity— what Beckett nicely calls "the plagiarism of oneself."[12] The problem, of course, is that Beckett's characters are often amnesiacs. They have no memory, neither voluntary nor involuntary. They have forgotten their name, what they were told just a moment before; they wander haphazardly along now unknown paths, losing little by little the thread of their speech. Like Molloy, Vladimir, or the voices in *That Time*, which get tangled in the threads of the past.

Furthermore, that memory does not allow the "redis-covery" of the past is also the case for Proust, Beckett claims in 1930. Even the famous "involuntary memory," that of the madeleine or Venice's uneven cobblestones, can ultimately bring nothing back to us but death. In the end, Beckett em-phasizes, Proust's work is not about rediscovering time; it is about abolishing it. Only the ecstasy of art can save us from time and death. Thus, in Proust's work, suggests Beckett, the past does not *pass*; it is never *surpassed*: it *amasses*. "Yesterday is not a milestone that has been passed but a daystone on the beaten track of the years, and irremediably part of us, within us, heavy and dangerous."[13]

This helps to explain the dust that slowly rises from floor to ceiling, piling up and covering everything at the end of *That Time*. The voices do not recall the past in a ret-rospective gesture by which it would be ordered and given meaning. It is a past in ruins, ever present, that piles up next to them, little by little covering them, and in which the characters, slowly decomposing and falling into ruin, fade and melt away. Consider "For to End Yet Again," "Ping," and "Lessness." Go back further yet to Molloy the decomposed cripple, Malone who never finishes dying, Mahood the pustule-covered skull; they all ultimately raise the same question as the narrator in *The Unnamable*: "why time doesn't pass, doesn't pass, from you, why it piles up all about you, instant on instant, on all sides, deeper and deeper, thicker and thicker, your time, others' time, the time of the ancient dead and the dead yet unborn, why it buries you grain by grain neither dead nor alive, with no memory of anything, no hope of anything, no knowledge of anything, no history and no prospects, buried under the seconds, saying any old thing, your mouth full of sand [. . .]."[14]

Uncertainty Principle

Deleuze was right when he said that in Beckett's work there is a "fantastic decomposition of self," "stench and agony included";[15] but it also must be made clear the extent to which Samuel Beckett brings the void "into play" (in every sense of the phrase),[16] which is to say the extent to which his work slowly but surely transforms the anguish of death into eroticization, the *jouissance* of limits. It's this question I would like to dwell on here in conclusion.

It is, then, a general principle of uncertainty regarding temporality that dominates the entire text of *That Time.* Everything is caught in an incessant movement, causing the points of reference to constantly shift: nothing is fixed, everything slides endlessly. Thus, the number eleven (the same eleven!) represents indiscriminately for voice A a tram number, a date (though, that said, this is not sure: "ten or eleven") and the age of a child ("eleven or twelve in the ruin on the flat stone . . ."). A temporal uncertainty obviously marks, as such, this world where all points of reference shift as one tries to pin them down, but there is also an uncertainty of space since the frame is ill-defined and open, and the limits blurred: the inside often turns itself into the outside. Hence the "character" of voice C, looking at the paintings in the museum where he has taken shelter from the rain ("till you hoisted your head and there before your eyes when they opened a vast oil black with age and dirt [. . .] behind the glass where gradually as you peered . . ." [389]) and who wonders if it is not perhaps of himself, this dirty portrait before which curious people pass without seeing it: "to say nothing of the loathsome appearance [. . .] all the eyes passing over you and through you like so much thin air" (394). Who, then, is looking at whom? Who is painting and who spectator? Where is the true, "real," world; where is the representation? Where is the limit?

After all, is it the Listener who breathes life into these voices, or do the voices invent and recite the Listener, hold him there, suspended between light and dark, sleep (eyes closed) and attentiveness (eyes open)? And what about us, the reader or spectator of the work: do we ultimately occupy such a clearly defined role? And what exactly are we watching and from what place? The Listener's face, according to the stage directions, is at once and paradoxically situated "10 feet above stage level" and with "long flaring white hair as if *seen from above* outspread" (my emphasis). In other words, it is seen at once from below and from above. It is a contradictory dual perspective that undeniably puts the spectator in a somewhat uncomfortable position. It is a little like the skull in "For to End Yet Again," seen from both above and below. That is to say that the spectator, here, has no unified point of view—nothing resembling the traditional Euclidean position of the viewer of a painting (and we know the importance of pictorial references in Beckett's theater), those laws of perspective established during the Renaissance and based on the unified vision of an immobile eye (the linear triangulation of space, focal points, vanishing lines). Here, on the contrary, the eye moves, and we are as though stretched between top and bottom, we, too, hanging in space, literally pulled out of our centered position as spectators. "Am I right in the centre?" asks Hamm regularly in *Endgame.* Here, the Listener, as the stage directions make clear, is "off centre." It is, then, a topological and deformable space, based on the notions of proximity and envelopment, independent of any fixed scale of measurement—i.e., non-Euclidean. And ourselves, the readers, as we read this text in which a Listener hears the noise of readers' breath and "turned pages" rising from the library, can we be certain that we are outside the text and not *within* it, turning the pages of the book we are in the process of reading?

It is this constant *passage* from outside to inside, interior to exterior, one voice to another that typifies the way this text works by shifts and echoes. The idea of passage is, however, for Beckett, always twofold. On the one hand, he plays on passage as uncertainty (who is speaking? where should one cut? what time?) or even anguish, but also, inversely, as *jouissance*, eroticization of limits and sensuality of language. The actor David Warrilow reminds us that, in *A Piece of Monologue*, the soliloquist twice describes how one has to position one's mouth and tongue in order to pronounce the word "birth": the tip of the tongue between the lips, a gentle, highly sensual feeling. The description, he underlines, is similar to the act of birth itself. It is for this reason that Samuel Beckett apparently said to him, "I don't think there will ever be a French version of this text. '*Naissance*' is the only French word for 'birth,' and the 'th' sound doesn't exist." In the end, of course, he did write a shorter French version. It was, remarks Warrilow, one of the rare occasions he struggled with the translation.[17]

Roland Barthes spoke of "writing aloud," that vocal writing that is "also what Artaud recommended," a writing carried by what Barthes calls "the *grain* of the voice," searching for "the language lined with flesh, a text where we can hear the grain of the throat, the patina of consonants, the voluptuousness of vowels, a whole carnal stereophony: the articulation of the body."[18] There is indeed in Beckett's writing

an undeniable voluptuousness of phonic, vocal, and jacula-
tory articulation, a *jouissance* of the continually reenacted
passage from inside to outside, from interior to exterior, of
orality. As such, it is hardly a coincidence that the mouth is
promoted to the rank of character in *Not I.* Remember the
reference in *Molloy* to "pure sounds, free of all meaning"
and the greedy love of words that saves the old Krapp from
mental death in *Krapp's Last Tape*: the sounds of "viduity"
and "spooool," uttered "with relish."

Fragile Lightness of Being

Over and above anguish, it is also this eroticization of
limits that is experienced by readers and listeners of *That
Time.* This is because, in order to read this text, one must
constantly reenact separation. We know what psychoanalysis can tell us about this playing with limits, and I refer
readers here to the works of Angela Moorjani,[19] for example. The text of *That Time,* beneath the trio of voices, is
indeed a single flow of words, a single breath given rhythm
by the noise of the Listener's respiration ("breath audible,
slow and regular"). The reader is called on throughout to
segment this text written without punctuation or capitals,
to separate the elements of speech—and we often hesitate,
do not know exactly where to cut, which limits to trace in
this hesitant and fluid syntax Beckett invents, a syntax that
leaves us as though unresolved between retrospection (to
go back and reread) and prospection (you must go on . . .
as the other says . . . forward!). In other words, meaning—
fragile and fleeting—forms only for a moment, and we
must seize it as though in mid-air, catch it between before
and after, past and future, memory and invention. What
we must experience with Beckett (rather than interpret) is
this: the fleeting and deformable nature of forms. Hence
this passage: "never another after that never looked back
after that was that the time . . . ," where one hesitates for

a second, wondering whether to cut between "that was" or "was that" ("after that was that the time" [390]). Here, again, is a minuscule chiasmus, reproducing in a *mise en abyme* that of the whole text. And this: "that kip on the front where you no she was with you."

For the final example I'd like to give, I had to look at the text in English before I could grasp the meaning of the French version (the poetic force of Beckettian ambiguities . . .). Voice B is speaking: "or alone in the same the same scenes making it up that way to keep it going keep it out on the stone alone on the end of the stone with the wheat and blue or the towpath alone on the towpath with the ghosts of the mules the drowned rat *or bird or whatever it was* [*ou l'oiseau qui sait bestiole quelconque*] floating off into the sunset till you could see it no more nothing stirring only the water and the sun going down . . ." (393; my emphasis). I had initially read the French text as "*l'oiseau qui sait* [bird who knows]." Who knows what? When I then read the English, however, the intended segmentation became clear: "*ou l'oiseau / qui sait / bestiole quelconque.*"

What does this constant reflection mean for Beckett: to be *passing*, in a temporary place, place without place, untenable, unstable? One might naturally arrive at a metaphysical or religious answer: it is the temporary sojourn in the Christian sense; we are all merely passing through on this earth; only the heavenly sojourn is eternal. So be it. Nevertheless, it seems to me that we might ascribe to it a more secular, existential, meaning. The subject Beckett calls ephectic (in *The Unnamable*) is a subject of uncertainty, an unstable subject ("I am . . . perhaps"). With Beckett, as we have seen, we doubt everything and, above all, the world and existence. We no long truly believe in any of it: life, death, eternity, the beyond, and so on. Hence the way his work resonates within us, his modernity. Beckett shares with a few other melancholic moderns this incredulity as to the reality of the existence of the world and the self. It is the link between man and the world that has been severed, said Deleuze.[20] Consequently, it is this link that must become the object of belief.

What does it mean "to believe in the link"? For Beckett, it might be to believe in the fragile, tenuous, and yet relentless vitality of writing, that thread, ever ready to break and yet continually woven again and again: *The Unnamable*'s "you must go on, I can't go on, I'll go on"; writing's exhausted and inexhaustible force of resistance. In *That Time*, the ego splits into distinct ages (childhood, middle age, and old age) that juxtapose, overlap, and echo each other without ever merging and uniting in a single story. What Beckett portrays here are shards of time without center, without chronology, but which coexist and link up here and there, at a distance. "*At the limit,*" as the expression goes—implying that it is always about to snap—*there is a link.*

What is it that we discover, then, as we travel through Beckett's universe, escaping with him the old order, that of belief in the narration—this retrospective story that is supposedly our own? It is that we, too, are perhaps made up of moving fragments only temporarily assembled, in a constant process of assembly and disassembly. This has nothing to do with biblical condemnation, come to us via Ecclesiastes ("for dust thou art, and unto dust shalt thou return"). With Beckett, we are no longer in the religious or depressive universe of the Fall. The dust is agitated by tiny movements tirelessly undone and reconnected by the writing. Thus, through reading it, everyone momentarily becomes like Watt, made up of millions of grains that slide or turn and remain suspended in the air . . .

The sudden lightness of it all . . . don't you think?

BLANCHOT HERO

[. . .] and the saint who formerly was "chary of speech"
in obedience to a commandment of silence could just be
recognised in the artist who schooled himself to silence
lest words should return him his discourtesy.
—James Joyce, Stephen Hero

The formulation is well known to readers of Blanchot in French: "Maurice Blanchot, novelist and critic. His life is wholly dedicated to literature and the silence which is proper to it."[1] Until his death, this succinct summation replaced the usual biographical introduction in the paperback versions of his books published in French. Whether one finds it artificial, even grandiloquent, or sees in it, on the contrary, the sign of an authentic greatness, it is for many of Blanchot's readers emblematic of the heroic standing he shaped for himself over time: that of the writer wedded, in life, to the annihilation that is writing, sculpting in the flesh his statue of the eternal and great dead writer ("infinitely dead," as he says of Orpheus, borrowing the term from Rilke). More fundamentally, this formulation can be seen to reveal the *heroic temptation* that doubtlessly never left Blanchot, in line with the positions he took up in the 1930s—not that this is evident in anything he explicitly stated, but it is, I believe, discernable in the insidious seductive power that the ideal of virile mastery and aristocratic elitism, the taste of greatness and asceticism, still held over him, as did, equally, the passion for the extreme and detestation of softness and moderates. Such was the psychical armor that at the same time—it goes without saying—allowed him to undertake the hazardous exploration of the nocturnal territories of madness and death.

The year 2007 was the centenary of Maurice Blanchot's birth. As with his death, four years earlier, the event sparked both fervent celebration and the return of old controversies. Primarily those well-founded accusations concerning Blanchot's proximity in the 1930s to the nationalist and racist Maurrassian extreme right[2] and the violence of his political articles in the antidemocratic press of the time, a press verging on the national revolutionary.[3] As has sometimes and quite rightly been pointed out, Blanchot's political engagements are indissociable from his engagement in writing. Before his political battles alongside communist intellectuals against the Algerian War, colonialism, and General de Gaulle, and before his enthusiastic participation in the May 1968 protests and his support for the Czechoslovakian resistance fighters opposing the Soviet Army: before all of that, Maurice Blanchot wrote regularly for extreme-right newspapers and journals. On this period of his life, he was never to say anything outright. A mere allusion now and again, most notably very late in his life in an article published in *Débat* in 1984, a short passage of which resonates as a painful reflection: "There would thus seem to be a moment, in every life, when the unjustifiable prevails and the incomprehensible is given its due," he writes, before adding, "A painful memory and a painful enigma."[4]

A further accusation (apparently on quite a different front) is frequently leveled at Blanchot by all those who clearly cannot stand his writing: that his work is deeply melancholic, despairing—in short, a vector of death; something toxic. Such a judgment attests at times to an almost phobic rejection; it is as though Blanchot's patient, meditative experiences, his long and tortuous reflections, his immersion into the disquieting depths of language,[5] provoked in many of these readers insufferable anguish—whence this inevitable defensive reflex. A common reaction is "Blanchot? No sense of humor!" Blanchot's humor is admittedly so subtle as to be almost undetectable, incomprehensible for many, as is that of Anne, ever silent, in *Thomas the Obscure*: "But her silence did not even have the right to silence, and through this absolute state were expressed at once the complete unreality of Anne and the unquestionable and indemonstrable presence of this unreal Anne, from whom there emanated, by this silence, a sort of terrible horror which one became uneasily conscious of" (*TO,* 68). An example would be the following, in a phrase he wrote about Rilke: "one sees clearly that he seeks to make of our end something other than an accident which would arrive from outside to terminate us hastily" (*SL,* 125). Or this, also in *The Space of Literature,* about the heroic death of the ancient Stoics: "when, upon seeing her husband, Caecina Poetus, hesitate, Arria plunges a dagger into her own breast, draws it back out, and offers it to him saying, 'It is not painful,' her steadiness—her stiffness—is impressive. Restraint is a feature of great and tranquil death scenes which gives pleasure" (*SL,* 100).

And yet Georges Poulet writes, "A desolate work, one of the saddest that exists in any literature," adding, "Fictional creation is, for Maurice Blanchot, the creation of nothing. His novel is an air bell, a machine to create the void."[6] Further to this cliché of nothingness, nihilism, or even negative theology in Blanchot's work, there is one final element that fueled the criticism: his progressive withdrawal from public life during the 1970s. Little by little, his illness abetting but not the sole cause, he made himself invisible and a recluse, communicating only through writing and distancing himself from the world in a manner that some judged aristocratic and supercilious, while friends and loyal followers recognized it as the persistent sign of an intransigent conception of writing. As they correctly pointed out, moreover, Blanchot continued writing, publishing, and contributing to public debate until nearly the very end of his life, which gives a very different image from the caricature sometimes presented of a writer already posthumous during his lifetime. Hence the following, in an article written not long after his death: "He is no more. And yet nothing has changed: be he dead or alive, whatever one writes on Maurice Blanchot is an obituary. The author of *Literature and the Right to Death* did not wait to die from his empirical death, at the age of 96, in order to disappear— and to make the necessary arrangements, as they say. His demanding and desolate work is, as is known, nothing but the endless rehashing of a never-ending suicide."[7]

The Last Writer

Can one deny, however—for the question must be raised here, even if it is of only limited significance—that Blanchot's writing does, at times, tend to go off on digressive tangents that might, quite understandably, annoy the reader? Certain affectations of his writing, too, sometimes verge on vain posturing, again with the potential to irritate (which is the same reproach, of course, addressed by many to Derrida's final work). One such example is found in the very last footnote, in italics, of *The Infinite Conversation*; the last words of an addendum withdrawn as quickly as it is made: "*I dedicate* (and disavow) *these uncertain pages to the books in which the absence of the book is already producing itself as promise in keeping its word; books written by—, but let no more than the lack of a name designate them here, for the sake of friendship*" (*IC*, 464).

And yet, there is a second, more fundamental question:

whether or not we are sensitive to the toxic tone of his books, can we deny that his conception of literature's *spectral* essence is the very basis of the extreme experience of writing (the "limit-experience," as he writes in *The Infinite Conversation*) to which Blanchot abandons himself? Is he not himself, as such, that *last writer*, who, like Orpheus, does not fear breaching the frontiers of death to confront the infernal powers? And what is it that he finds there? That which he did not know he was searching for: "the mystery of writing."[8] Suffice it to say, on this path death is infinitely subtle; far from the insurmountable barriers reputed to divide the dead and the living, it no longer represents the absolute antithesis of life. Shattering our overly simplistic oppositions, it is this very idea that Blanchot finds in the pre-Socratic philosophers, particularly in the work of Heraclitus the Obscure. Each of Heraclitus's sentences is a cosmos, he writes, in which Day and Night, Yes and No, Life and Death, switch places and change function: "this offers us the remarkable formulation 'living death,' 'dying life,' which is found in several fragments. Entering into composition with the couple 'men-gods,' such formulations give us this extreme movement of language: 'Immortal Mortals, Mortal Immortals: living their death and dying their life'" (*IC*, 442).

Similarly, what Orpheus discovers in the underworld is not a living Eurydice, as Blanchot points out in his tireless rereading of the myth, but the "presence of her infinite absence": he finds "living in her the plenitude of her death" (*SL*, 172). One glimpses in this wonderful turn of phrase that the work is constantly slipping away, carrying us beyond all desire to grasp it. This slipping away, the Blanchotian detour,[9] is, then, equivalent to the Beckettian creative failure. The same command is endlessly repeated: "Fail better," says Beckett; write to "decreate" yourself. Undo the work, replies Blanchot, write *the ungrounding* [*l'effondrement*].

The very bottom, the ungrounding, belongs to art: this
ground that is sometimes the absence of foundation, the
pure void bereft of importance, and *sometimes* that upon
which a foundation can be given, but it is also *always
at the same time* one and the other, the intertwining of
the Yes and of the No, the ebb and flow of the essential ambiguity. And that is why all works of art and all
literary works seem to leave comprehension behind and
yet seem never to reach it, so that it must be said of them
that they are always understood too much and always
too little." (*SL*, 238 [transl. modified])

That which Blanchot patiently elaborates in his writing is
not therefore the absence of the work (a simply negative
movement) but, in a more complex way, the *unworking*
[*désœuvrement*], that force of creative dissolution in which
a subject-becoming-writer never ceases to die. Put as clearly as possible: *writing, for Blanchot, is a form of heroism.*
And what is the definition of heroism? Not self-sacrifice
in the face of death (that commonplace of the warrior
hero) but another understanding, infinitely more subtle,
even mad (Marguerite Duras, of course, noted Blanchot's
proximity to madness), which he came to formulate little
by little as he plunged ever deeper into his writing, like Orpheus into the underworld: the heroism of an impersonal
death. What Blanchot refutes is indeed the entire individ-
ualist and humanist tradition that makes death something
one can *appropriate.* Two of the most eloquent examples
of this in the Western imaginary are that artists live on in
their work and that everyone can make death *their own.* In
both cases, it is the same illusion: that one can make death
one's work.

Blanchot contrasts the great figures of Orpheus and
Kafka against this first notion, that of the creator who believes to have vanquished death by making *their name* an

immortal name: what one wants, he writes, "is not to sub-sist in the leisurely eternity of idols, but to change, to disap-pear in order to cooperate in the universal transformation: to act anonymously" (*SL,* 94). Hence Orpheus metamor-phosing to become "the infinitely dead" that the power of song makes of him (*SL,* 142).[10] Hence, too, the "volatization of the very fact of death," which Rilke discovers following his mystical experiences at Capri and Duino and which re-mains apparent in his *Sonnets to Orpheus*: "After having, at first, made art 'the road toward myself,' he feels increas-ingly that this road must lead to the point where, within myself, I belong to the outside. It leads me where I am no longer myself, where if I speak it is not I who speak, where I cannot speak. To encounter Orpheus is to encounter this voice which is not mine, this death which becomes song, but which is not my death, even though I must disappear in it more profoundly" (*SL,* 155–56).

The second notion, that of heroic suicide, is found, as we have seen, in the Stoics, but it is more widely apparent in the voluntary death of those "lofty men" who die with "their eyes gazing steadfastly beyond the clouds," as the poet Jean-Paul Richter wrote (*SL,* 111). Again, says Blan-chot, we must forget the individualistic conception of the nineteenth century that one can "die an individual death, still oneself at the very last, [. . .] be an individual right up to the end, unique and undivided" (*SL,* 122). Another reference to Rilke, who refused to "die like a fly in the hum of mindlessness and nullity" and for a time wished to make death *his own,* believing it might be the moment of his greatest authenticity, before he was able to get through his anguish of an anonymous death. For Blanchot, the major flaw in this belief in the greatness of a voluntary death is that, in delivering oneself up to it, one believes to be master of one's own fate, when one is in fact refusing "to reach the pure center where we would find our bearings again in that

which exceeds us" (*SL,* 121). This is what Nietzsche wished
to communicate through the voice of Zarathustra: "Man is
something that must be overcome" (*SL,* 119). It is a phrase,
says Blanchot, that one must not interpret as the illusion
of attaining something beyond man; man has nothing to
attain if he is that which he exceeds. Such is Nietzsche's
thought.

Here, however, precisely lies the danger of Blanchot's position, *for the very reason* of its irrefutable greatness. Orpheus the poet, or Orpheus-Blanchot, that hero who passes
beyond the law and confronts the terrifying forces of nocturnal dissolution, is also he who finds in himself, and in
his art, that which "transforms powerlessness into power"
(*BC,* 221). Even in taking care not to harden Blanchot's
stance, there is no denying that force and power are what is
at stake here, in the paradoxical (and fantasmatic) idealized
all-powerfulness bestowed upon the writer through his position of *triumphant powerlessness.* For lack of space, we
shall not detail here all the difficulties raised by similar and
frequently ill-understood notions, such as the Nietzschean
overman or the "super-fascism" that was somewhat pre-
cipitously attributed to Bataille; but the possible excesses
of this superhuman idolization cannot be ignored. Already
during the war, when he published *Faux Pas* in 1943—the
date is, of course, not coincidental—Blanchot wrote the
following: "The writer is summoned by his anguish to an
actual sacrifice of himself. [. . .] He must be destroyed in an
act that actually puts him in play. *The exercise of his ability*
[*pouvoir*] forces him to immolate this ability [*pouvoir*]" (*FP,*
5; my emphasis). And again, in 1948, in that famous text
"Literature and the Right to Death," he wrote: "The writer senses that he is in the grasp of an *impersonal power*
that does not let him either live or die: the irresponsibility

he cannot surmount becomes the expression of that death without death which awaits him at the edge of nothingness [. . .]. The writer who writes a work eliminates himself as he writes that work and at the same time *affirms himself* in it" (*WF,* 340; my emphasis).

Beyond the Bataillean resonances in all of this (expenditure, sacrifice), this dizzying ebb and flow between power and powerlessness is not without its risks. Let the movement stop and everything becomes fixed; the vanishing of the self turns to triumph; the heroic posture solidifies into a pose: I embody the Literary hero. Given this, we ought not to be surprised to find Blanchot penning certain phrases that ring with a bizarrely warlike tone. Take, for example, this praise of the "great virile creators" (*SL,* 53; translation modified), the repeated mention of "noble and rare thoughts" (*FP,* 5), and the heroic sacrifice of self through writing: "When we admire the tone of a work, when we respond to its tone as to its most authentic aspect, what are we referring to? Not to style, or to the interest and virtues of the language, but to this silence precisely, *this vigorous force* [*cette force virile*] by which the writer, having been deprived of himself, having renounced himself, has in this effacement nevertheless maintained the *authority of a certain power*: the power decisively to be still, so that in this silence what speaks without beginning of end might take on form, coherence, and sense" (*SL,* 27; my emphasis).

Giving Death a Voice

By a similar derivation that the work could not fail to engender, no doubt, this hagiographic image of Blanchot the "hero of Literature" was to find itself bolstered by many readers. Proof, if one is needed, of the difficulty of *maintaining* the unstable heroism of the impersonal. For this reason, one is all the more grateful for the salutary, iconoclastic contribution of Catherine Malabou at the "*Passions de la littérature*" symposium, which took place at Louvain-la-Neuve University in 1995.[11] The devastatingly ironic pastiche she presented of Blanchot's *The Instant of My Death* and of the commentary (both admirable and brimming with admiration) Jacques Derrida had just written on it, *Demeure: Fiction and Testimony,* gleefully made the statue of the hero (of the *two* heroes: of writing and of thought) wobble. Imagining Blanchot's account as though written by the Russian who perhaps saved the narrator's life, she proceeds to irreverently dethrone—in the carnivalesque sense of the word—the narrator of Blanchot's neither true nor false account, that aristocrat ready to die a hero, though ultimately spared by the Russians, and thus forever removed from "the world of mere mortals." And so, she remarks with humor, "No war will ever weaken feudalism." At the end, drawn up alongside Blanchot's text, is the great figure of Derrida: "and I consider with despairing fascination," concludes the Russian, his speech delivered by Catherine Malabou, "the French writer and philosopher of great repute," who stands now before the audience at Louvain-La-Neuve, he, too, "tall and upright, for so long, like a lord venerated by all." One can imagine the burst of laughter (or dismayed silence?) that would have (ought to have?) erupted from the assembly at Louvain-La-Neuve.

If indeed the writer is he or she who speaks *on behalf of death* (gives it their voice, speaks in this place that does not take place[12]), as I believe Blanchot suggests, then there are two characters we should not be surprised to encounter in his work, one terrifying and the other held in contempt: the Commander and General de Gaulle, who, setting themselves up in their full calcified stature before the symbolic son (Kafka, Orpheus, Don Juan, Blanchot, and so on), bar his access to living death. Both embody the frozen and definitively sterile death, "the night of stone" in which writing becomes mired and revolt is lost. De Gaulle, the politically dead "spectral old man," the "presence of petrified humanity" (*PW,* 90), came to epitomize during the events of May '68 all of Blanchot's revolutionary rage against the Father, the Fatherland, and the State.

> If today there is a politically dead man in this country,
> it is the one who carries—does he carry it?—the title
> of President of the Republic, a Republic to which he is
> just as foreign as he is to any living political future. He is
> an actor, playing a role borrowed from the oldest story,
> just as his language is the language of a role, an imitated
> speech at times so anachronistic that it seems to have
> been always posthumous. [. . .] And this dead man,
> unaware that he is dead, is impressive with the great
> stature of death, with the dead obstinacy that passes for
> authority, and at times with the obnoxious, distinguished
> vulgarity that signifies the dissolution of being-dead.
> (*PW,* 90)

Would Blanchot be speaking, unconsciously, of himself here—as would mockingly suggest his detractors? Quite probably . . . but at the same time, and in a more complex way, both De Gaulle and the Commander present a horrifying portrayal of the dead Father, the powerless *père-pierre* [father-stone] who symbolizes the "impossibility— the abyss of non-power, the icy, frozen excess of the *other* night" (*IC,* 190). In what is a clearly aggressive projection, these two characters represent paternal impotence, the obliteration of his power over the son (Blanchot, of course, makes numerous references to Kafka's *Letter to His Father*), the final erection of a now-petrified phallus. It is a final ironic subversion: every hero is impotent . . . in potentia.

What should we conclude from all of this? Blanchot writes that literature's "lack of being (of intelligible reality) causes it to refer to an existence that is still inhuman" (*WF,* 339). How better to say that what is experienced, by both the writer and the reader, is just as much anguish as an incontestable *exhilaration of the inhuman* (or "dishuman" [*déshumain*], to borrow again Pierre Fédida's term).[13] "In the poem it is not any particular individual who risks himself alone, or a particular mind that is exposed to the touch and the burn of darkness. The risk is more essential. It is the danger of dangers by which, each time, the essence of language is radically placed in doubt. To risk language: this is one of the forms of this risk. [. . .] The work draws light from the dark; it is a relation with what admits of no relations; it encounters being before the encounter is possible and where truth lacks. This is the essential risk. Here we reach the abyss" (*SL,* 238–39).

The ideal reader of *Finnegans Wake*—as Joyce envisaged him or her—would be an insomniac.[14] Readers of Blanchot require, for their part, no doubt, a certain psychological plasticity, an aptitude for temporarily putting aside our fixed representations, a flexibility of identification—a predilection for the "dishuman," perhaps, on condition that we understand the positive implications of the term: the wonder of temporarily freeing ourselves from so-called human limits. In this sense, Pierre Fédida was right to underline that "Blanchot's writing invites us to move away from a representation of sexual identities" (which is the principal difference between him and Bataille). This is why, in *The Most High,* the body is clamor, and the erotic scene lacks the support of characters; one can identify neither man nor woman. Psychoanalysis, he concludes, does not give enough credence to the idea that "sexual experience is a loss of identity."[15] As is the reading of Blanchot.

BLANCHOT'S ANAGRAMS

A Reading of *Thomas the Obscure*

The old, dangerous fever of the anagrams has her in its grip. She creates one after another. Dangerous for her because once again she shuts herself off completely from her surroundings.

—Unica Zürn, *The Man of Jasmine*

The Breath of Letters

One day we shall have to investigate why, with Maurice Blanchot and certain others, reading became in the twentieth century an experience of the extreme. No longer simply the innocent (or inflammatory) pastime through which you feel by projection, experience by identification, and live vicariously—that transplant of the imaginary Proust still describes, evoking young Marcel's afternoons spent reading in Combray: "these afternoons were crammed with more dramatic events than occur, often, in a whole lifetime"[1]—reading was to transmute, rather, into the difficult yet exhilarating ordeal of which Bataille speaks in *Inner Experience*: "I write for one, who, entering into my book, would fall into it as into a hole, who would never again get out."[2] While those who venture into Blanchot's texts are not required, unlike the readers of Bataille, to go quite as far as the temporary "loss of self" in ecstasy or sacrifice that the latter describes (and Bataille does, no doubt, *describe* this more than he *writes* it), it is nevertheless a strange trajectory that awaits them.

Let us conjecture that what *Thomas the Obscure* both writes and recounts is precisely this: an almost mad experience of the life and death of words that draws writer and reader alike into an endless turmoil, disrupting their every point of reference. That the book opens with an account of Thomas's immersion in a sea as inviting as it is menacing is, of course, not fortuitous. Reading resembles, here, a sometimes suffocating dive into a moving space, where one is in turn absorbed and thrown back out, at times included, at others brutally expelled. Resuscitating letters, breathing movement back into words, the writer and reader both experience the endless process of death and resurrection that Blanchot sees at work in all literary writing. The following lines from his seminal article of 1947, "Literature and the Right to Death," serve as a succinct summary of writing as an interminable process: literature "knows it is the movement through which whatever disappears keeps appearing. When it names something, whatever it designates is abolished; but whatever is abolished is also sustained, and the thing has found a refuge (in the being which is the word) rather than a threat" (*WF*, 329).

Taking up more than once, in this way, as much Mallarmé's evocation of the absence of the named thing in the word[3] as Hegel's qualification of the first name as a murder, Blanchot transposes the well-known formulation of *The Phenomenology of Spirit*: "In speech what dies is what gives life to speech; speech is the life of that death, it is 'the life that endures death and maintains itself in it'" (*WF*, 327). Which is to say that, contrary to a common preconception, writing, for Blanchot, never becomes a dead letter [*lettre morte*].[4] Consequently, what is played out in *Thomas the Obscure* is an inexhaustible and paradoxical revitalization

of death; such that the statement that opens the story—
"The book was rotting on the table" (*TO*, 26)—is reversed.

It is easy to understand the irritation that some have felt
in reading Blanchot's "philosophico-poetic speculations,"
an annoyance echoed by the philosopher Jacques Rancière.
By not hesitating to compare the experience of reading *The
Space of Literature* to the initiatory ordeal faced by Orpheus in his descent to the underworld, Blanchot did, indeed, lay himself open to the criticism many made of him
of being, like Bataille, a "new mystic," a priest transforming
literature into a sacred ritual and surrounding himself, in
his vocation of silence, with a few sycophantic followers all
too ready to form a sect. As Rancière points out, Blanchot
has often been seen as the emblematic figure of a modern
tendency toward the absolutization of art inherited from
the German romantics—that sanctification of literature
that has equally been embodied in France by Flaubert and
his "book about nothing" and Mallarmé and his project of a
writing proper to the Idea. The name Blanchot has, as such,
become at times synonymous with "literature's claim to be
an unheard-of and radical exercise of thought and language, perhaps even a social calling and priesthood."[5] But
is it indeed to the cult of an immobile essence of literary
creation that Blanchot's work is dedicated? Can we legiti-
mately qualify as "metaphors" those very real movements
that Blanchot breathes into the very materiality of word
and syntax? Far from negative theology's "ineffable," with
which he is often associated, and just as equally far from
the romantic idealization of the poetic Verb, Blanchot was,
in fact, to constantly insist on the physical reality of the
body of words and their tangible and perceptible effects:

> Take the trouble to listen to a single word: in that word
> nothingness is struggling and toiling away, it digs tire-
> lessly, doing its utmost to find a way out, nullifying what

encloses it—it is infinite disquiet, formless and nameless
vigilance. Already the seal which held this nothingness
within the limits of the word and within the guise of its
meaning has been broken; now there is access to other
names, names which are less fixed, still vague, more capable of adapting to the savage freedom of the negative
essence—they are unstable groups, no longer terms but
the movement of terms, an endless sliding of "turns of
phrase" which do not lead anywhere. [. . .]

Then what hope do I have of attaining the thing I push
away? My hope lies in *the materiality of language,* in the
fact that *words are things, too,* are a kind of nature—this
is given to me and gives me more than I can understand.
[. . .] A name ceases to be the ephemeral passing of
nonexistence and becomes a *concrete ball,* a *solid mass
of existence*; [. . .] Everything physical takes precedence:
rhythm, weight, mass, shape, and then the paper on
which one writes, the trail of the ink, the book. Yes,
happily language is a thing [. . .]. The word acts not as
an ideal force but as an obscure power, as an incarnation
that coerces things, makes them *really* present outside of
themselves. (*WF,* 326–328; my emphasis)

It is possible, then, that with Blanchot, as with many other
modern writers, reading is less a matter of an imaginary
appropriation than our ability to cope with the effects of
more or less violent and destructuring affects produced
in us by the text. In other words, readers must be able *to
not resist* the real transferential effects that the writing has
on them; better still would be that they demonstrate a certain *aptitude for disassociation*—a quality required, as we
know, just as much in psychoanalysts as analysands. Disso-
ciate and associate, undo and redo: such is the movement
entailed by Blanchot's writing and the reading of it. Indeed,
we shall privilege the term *disassociation* over that of *de-*

construction to designate this dynamic of affects, this trajectory of the forces of the drive at work in the space that Blanchot calls "literary" but which is clearly not so dissimilar from what Freud calls "analytic."[6] This is also to suggest that deconstruction no doubt partook of a certain aversion to psychoanalysis, as is revealed here and there by its resistance to take into account what writing owes to the power of the affect. This is made all the more manifest, moreover, by the facility with which some of deconstruction's disciples abandon themselves to the excesses of a writing that, more ludic than interpretative, veers quickly to a mere play on words, in much the same manner as the stylistic play characteristic of the heirs of a late and diluted Lacanianism.

Whether a homage to disjunctive force or not, the very title of the book clearly alludes to Heraclitus, whose name appears in Blanchot's work multiple times. Indeed, we have not sufficiently emphasized the profound link between Heraclitus, the model poet-philosopher, and the dissociated writing-reading of *Thomas the Obscure.* Consider this, from *The Infinite Conversation*: "Heraclitus the Obscure: so he has been qualified since ancient times [. . .] with the resolute aim of making answer to one another in writing [. . .] the obscurity of language and the clarity of things, mastery over the double sense of words and the secret of the dispersion of appearances: in other words, perhaps, *dis-course and discourse*" (*IC,* 87; my emphasis). Heraclitus is he who does not fear confronting that disparity he calls Difference and which plays on the retained interval, or tension, between disaccord and accord. Heraclitus is, as such, a model of what Thomas should be—Thomas being, here, another name for the reader.

Kafkian Metamorphoses

Although *Thomas the Obscure* is known to be a veiled tribute to Kakfa's *Metamorphoses,* the book does not so much

recount the myth or fable of Thomas's transformations—
Thomas being the new Gregor Samsa—as enact these latter
in its very writing, thereby implicating reading itself in the
infinite divagations and creeping of language. *Metamorphosis* is, then, a key word, not only occurring numerous
times[7] within the text but also being performed. The final
chapter is, as a result, the great chapter of metamorphoses,
of chrysalises becoming butterflies, the green caterpillar
becoming a sphinx moth (*TO*, 113) and, beyond that, of
infinitely reiterated shifts and slides—a metaphor for the
impossible exit from the world:

> "The ideal of color spread out across the fields. Across
> the transparent and empty sky extended the ideal of
> light." (*TO*, 113)
>   "Birds splashed with color, chosen to be the repertory
> of shades, rose up, presenting red and black to the void.
> Drab birds, designated to be the conservatory of music
> without notes, sang the absence of song." (*TO*, 114)

Further yet, the space of the entire book reads as a recy-
cling of quotations and metamorphoses of deformed and
reworked sentences, with its writing being just as canni-
balistic as is the reading that absorbs, assimilates, and
transforms: Pascal, Dante, Artaud, Kant, and Racine are all
tossed in somewhere or other.[8] All reading is devoration—
this is the central theme of the book's fourth chapter: to
devour is to "bring [. . .] into the deepest possible intimacy
with [oneself]" (*TO*, 28). And what is it that Thomas finds
in this intimacy, at the very heart of the word "devoration"?
The word "rat." "[H]e felt himself bitten or struck, he could
not tell which, by what seemed to him to be a word, but
resembled rather a giant rat, an all-powerful beast with
piercing eyes" (*TO*, 28).
     Let us remind ourselves of the passage. Thomas is read-
ing quietly, devouring a book with his eyes: "He was read-

ing with unsurpassable meticulousness and attention. In relation to every symbol, he was in the position of the male praying mantis about to be devoured by the female. They looked at each other. The words, coming forth from the book which was taking on the power of life and death, exercised a gentle and peaceful attraction over the glance which played over them" (*TO*, 25). In a series of successive inversions that gradually build up, Thomas devours a book with his eyes, devours the eyes of a book, and is devoured by a book's eyes: "he was perceived by the very quick [*l'intime*] of the word"; "he perceived all the strangeness there was in being observed by a word as if by a living being"; "the words were already taking hold of him and beginning to read him" (*TO*, 25–26). With that, Thomas transforms into a word, becomes text; he is literally the text he is reading: "For hours he remained motionless, with, from time to time, the word 'eyes' in place of his eyes: he was inert, captivated and unveiled" (*TO*, 26).

It is later that the rat takes hold of him. Before that, Thomas himself has had to mutate into vermin. "There he was on the floor, writhing, reentering himself and then leaving again. He crawled sluggishly [. . .]. He stuck his head under the bed, in a corner full of dust, resting among the rejectamenta as if in a refreshing place where he felt he belonged more properly than in himself" (*TO*, 28). This is reminiscent of Gregor Samsa hidden beneath his bed: "Long trails of dirt lined the walls, here and there lay heaps of dust and filth. At first, when his sister arrived, Gregor would station himself at particularly glaring corners of that sort [. . .]."[9]

Kafka is omnipresent in *Thomas the Obscure,* just as he is in all of Blanchot's work. Proof of this is that key sentence, which he reworks into a leitmotif, on the shift in Kafka's work from "I" to "He"—the discovery, in other words, of the impersonality of the subject of writing. An example can be found in *The Space of Literature*: "Kafka remarks, with surprise, with enchantment, that he has entered into literature as soon as he can substitute 'He' for 'I'" (*SL*, 26). It is a fundamental "transformation," writes Blanchot, by which we are to understand "a metamorphosis." He reinterprets the idea in *Thomas the Obscure*: "while, perched upon his shoulders, the word *He* and the word *I* were beginning their carnage" (*TO*, 26). This is a phrase that acquires its full meaning only when considered in relation to the first version of *Thomas the Obscure*, written in 1941: "In the inexplicable state that he found himself in, while the word *He* and the word *I* climbed up him like monstrous *cockroaches* and, perching upon his shoulders, began their interminable carnage."[10] In this version, Samsa, the Kafkian cockroach, is more explicitly implied. Although the final lines of the recit ("he threw himself into it, but sadly, desperately, as if the shame had begun for him" [*TO*, 117]) undoubtedly evoke the end of Kafka's *The Trial* ("it was as if the shame of it should outlive him"), they also clearly allude to the process of infinite metamorphosis of lives and deaths that Blanchot sees at work in the story of Gregor Samsa. "Gregor's state is the state of the being who cannot depart from existence; for him, to exist is to be condemned to falling continually back into existence" (*WF*, 9). The curse of metamorphosis is, then, the grotesque, laughable, condemnation that strikes Gregor-Thomas: "the shame of an endless existence" (*TO*, 91). This same idea, it should be noted, is developed by Emmanuel Levinas—whose proximity to Blanchot is shown here again—in his work *On Escape*, written at the same time Blanchot was writing the first version of *Thomas the Obscure*. For Levinas, the need for escape is a similar aspiration to exit a certain *definition* of our being, to escape from that nausea, that shame of being *riveted to oneself*: "A quest for the way out, this is in no sense a nostalgia for death because death is not an exit, just as it is not a solution. The ground of this theme is constituted—if one will pardon the neologism—by the need for *excendence.*"[11]

Metamorphosis is, then, torture and twisting, a sign of the torment that, Blanchot observes, equally manifests itself in the tortuous syntax of Kakfa's *Diaries,* with its quest toward the infinite regression of words and the instability of affirmations withdrawn almost as soon as they are made: "It is impossible to find out what face the thought turns toward us, it turns toward and away so much, as if, like a weight hanging by a string, its only object were to reproduce its *torsion*" (*WF,* 23; my emphasis).

Giving Body to Death

There is, then, no story to *Thomas the Obscure.* It doesn't recount Thomas's march toward inexistence, Anne's death without death or the infinity of movements that make any death temporary or impossible. Nor does it recount the transformation of a character (Thomas becoming a rat, Anne becoming a spider) but, rather, it makes this a subject of experimentation, rendering its existence palpable to us and making us fully experience it. As we progress through the text, there is a constant probing of copies, mirrors, and the reversibility of situations: to see / to be seen, to eat / to be eaten, to enter / to exit . . . The final metamorphosis of the metamorphosis is the book's reading proceeding letter by letter, with the words being opened up and the letters freed from their ties by a dissociative power that thereby *anagrammatizes* space. Blanchot retains from Mallarmé's project of the *Book* the fluid indecision and the mobility of separated pages evading the linearity of sense and reading. What he admires in *Un coup de dés* [*A Throw of the Dice*] is the invention of a new space combining "the greatest dispersion" and a tension capable of "*gathering* infinite diversity" (*BC,* 234; original emphasis). From the Mallarméan program, the madness of which fascinated him (along with

Kafka and Rilke, Mallarmé is his greatest inspiration), he garners not only the "extreme capacity for rupture" and the dissemination of syllables but equally reading's spacing and infinite movement as that supplanting both authorial and readerly individuality: "the book, unfolded and refolded, scattering and being gathered back together, shows that it has no substantial reality: it is never there, endlessly to be unmade while it is made" (*BC,* 266).

What of Blanchot's anagrams? We are aware of his penchant for graphic play and word puzzles. As Christophe Bident notes, "*Thomas* begins with the end of *Blanchot* and ends with the start of *Maurice.* In fact, the book's whole title, almost to the letter, is a cryptogram of *Maurice Blanchot.*"[12] We hardly need remind ourselves of the quasi-puns that constitute the surnames of certain characters in *Le Très Haut* [*The Most High*]: Sorge, the narrator, refers to Heideggerian "care"; Dorte alludes to death; Bouxx to books; Kraff, the prisoner writing his journal, is a remote Kafka; and so on. Nor do we need to dwell on those titles that are as distant echoes of one another: *Faux Pas* (1943), *La Part du Feu* (1949), *Le Pas au delà* (1973) (*Faux Pas, The Part of Fire,* and *The Step Not Beyond,* as they appear in translation). With regard to *Faux Pas,* the title of which equally plays on the misstep it performs, the legend also has it that it was inspired, in truncated form, by the title of Charles Plisnier's work *Faux Passeports,* which Blanchot reviewed in 1937 for the journal *L'Insurgé.*

A careful reading of *Thomas the Obscure,* the details of which it would be pointless to reproduce here, quickly brings to light a strange mobilization of the words' letters in continuation of the work of the metamorphoses identified above. Let us remind ourselves of that hallucinatory reading scene in chapter 4 in which the words became living and "in turn contained other words, like a procession of angels opening out into the infinite to the very eye of the absolute" (*TO*, 25). Blanchot's reader, if he or she, too, does not want to leave the book to "rot on the table," is very quickly caught up in the intense movement of dissociation, dispersion, and metamorphosis that troubles the text, a movement that, somewhere between Kafka and Mallarmé, renders the reading of *Thomas the Obscure* an irrefutable challenge. Blanchot, in his reading of *Coup de dés,* reminds us that Mallarmé's genius was to have invented a space requiring a reading that oscillates between the analysis of detail and an overall vision: "The literary work is suspended there between its visible presence and its readable presence: musical score or painting that must be read and poem that must be seen. Thanks to this oscillating alternation, it tries to enrich analytic reading by global and simultaneous vision, and also to enrich static vision by the dynamism of the play of optical movements. Finally, it contrives to place itself at the point of intersection where hearing is seeing and reading, but places itself also at that point where, no junction made, the poem occupies only the central void that represents the future of exception" (*BC,* 240–41).

Indeed, what is required here is the correct reading distance, somewhere between dissociation and relinking, between the dissemination of signs and their fleeting recomposition in words, sentences, and discourse. If the distance is too great, the book remains alien, unreadable; too small and the writing decomposes, crumbles into disparate series of syllabic or phonic fragments, where the book threatens, once again, to rot and organically decompose, to be struck by a gangrene of verbal and phrasal tissue.

A few examples should suffice. Between the first chapter (Thomas's bathing in some sort of great, primordial sea, that of cosmic myths evoking the quest for the origin of language) and chapter 4 (reading), there is more than one parallel to be drawn. Consider their respective *incipits*: "Thomas *sat* down and *looked at* the sea. He remained *motionless* [. . .], he *stayed* there, obstinately, his *eyes fixed* on the bodies" (*TO,* 7) becomes in chapter 4: "Thomas *stayed* in his room to read. He was *sitting* [. . .], so deep in concentration that he *did not make a move* [. . .]. They *looked at* each other" (*TO,* 25). To this apparent immobility there corresponds, in fact—beneath the surface of the sea and book, in the invisible depths of words—tiny dissociative movements of letters that set them in motion, make them invert themselves and pass into each other, engendering thereby that inexhaustible life that, in language, makes death impossible. Hence, in the first chapter, the word *nage* [swim] opens up into *nuage* [cloud], *rivage* [shore], *nageoire* [fin], *dégage* [free], *breuvage* [brew], *voyage* [journey], *visage* [face], and *vague* [wave]. In chapter 4, *nage* is anagrammatized and metamorphoses into *ange* [angel], which in turn becomes *étrange* [strange], *carnage* [carnage], *ange noir* [dark angel], *agonie* [agony], and so on: words "contained other words, like a procession of *angels* [*anges*] opening out into the infinite" (*TO,* 25), "while, perched upon his shoulders, the word *He* and the word *I* were beginning their *carnage*, there remained within his person which was already deprived of its senses obscure words, *disembodied* souls and *angels* of words [*paroles obscures, âmes* désincarnées *et* anges *de mots*], which were exploring him deeply" (*TO,* 26).[13]

One might find somewhat excessive my remarking that this last phrase ("*obscures, âmes* [. . .] *des mots*") again contains an anagram of the title: *Thomas l'Obscur*. As one might my noting the relationship between *agonie* ("*son corps subissait une agonie* [his body endured an agony]" [*TO,* 28]) and *ange noir* ("*elle était presque belle pour cette sorte d'ange noir* [it was almost beautiful for this dark angel]" [*TO,* 28]), which transits through the implied *agôn*

[agon] of the *lutte* [struggle/conflict] ("*cette lutte était hor-rible pour l'être couché par terre* [this struggle was terrible for the being lying on the ground]," "*son corps, après tant de luttes, devint entièrement opaque* [his body, after so many struggles, became entirely opaque]" [*TO*, 28–29]). More-over, amid the multitude of further examples throughout the text, one might pick up on the following anagram of *grande* and *danger*: "Anne had a few days of *great* [*grand*] happiness. [. . .] For her, he was suddenly a being she pos-sessed without *danger* [*danger*]. If she took hold of him, it was with the *greatest* [*plus grande*] freedom. [. . .] which permitted her to treat this *strange* [*étrange*] body as if it be-longed to her [. . .]. But she saw in him only a futile mouth, *empty glances* [*regards légers*]" (*TO*, 47).

Or further on: "*Je me trouvai avec deux* visages *collés l'un contre l'autre. Je ne cessai de toucher à deux* rivages. [. . .] *c'est à cette partie perdue dans un constant* naufrage *que je dus ma direction* [. . .] *au lieu de se* dégrader . . . [I found myself with two *faces*, glued one to the other. I was in constant contact with two *shores*. [. . .] it was to this part, lost in a constant *shipwreck*, that I owed my direction [. . .] rather than becoming *degraded* . . .]" (*TO*, 96–97). The question this prompts is that of how far we can take this painstaking analysis of the flurry of recurrent syllables as they become isolated and seem everywhere to hollow out words, dissociating them from themselves and opening up the reading to a clandestine proliferation that had previ-ously gone unnoticed. Is this the reading required by Blan-chot, the writer who describes Thomas immobile and fas-cinated, reading "with unsurpassable meticulousness and attention" (*TO*, 25)? Why not this, for example: "The man immersed in the waves [*vagues*] piled up by the absence of flood spoke to his horse [*cheval*] in a dialogue consisting of a single voice" (*TO*, 115). What is the reason for this horse, which has suddenly popped up out of nowhere, if it is not

to point out, undo and retie an unseen link between the
*che**val*** and the **va***gue*?

There is no point in listing further examples that anyone
who does not resist this dissociated reading could easily
find for themselves. We might note here, however, the anagram of this monstrous *être* [being], this *être* of language
that little by little disseminates and propagates itself: "*et
qui néanmoins l'empli**ssait** de* **terr***eur et qu'il sentai***t errer**
*dans l'**aire** de sa solitude. Toute la nuit, tout le jour ayant
veillé avec* **cet être***, comme il cherchait le repos, brusque-
ment, il fut averti qu'un autre avait remplacé le premier . . .*
[and which nevertheless filled him with terror as he sensed
it wandering about in the region of his solitude. Having
stayed up all night and all day with this being, as he tried
to rest he was suddenly made aware that a second had
replaced the first . . .]" (*TO*, 27).[14] We would be wrong, I
believe, to interpret this as a poetic use of speech in the
ornamental, decorative, or musically rhythmic sense, or as
a pure play on signifiers. It is my view that what we must
see and hear in this is the inscription of the organic and
atomic dissemination of letters through which Blanchot
attempts to seize the murmur of language. Let us elucidate
the point. Thomas is also a single-celled organism, a protoplasm, a paramecium: "Under the giant microscope, he
turned himself into an enterprising mass [*il se faisai***t amas**
entreprenant] of cilia and vibrations" (*TO*, 8). Between
Thomas and Tamas, are we also to identify the anagram of
Atome [atom]? Toward the end of the story, in that strange
city in the form of a sea that rises around Anne, the flow
of time is reversed: "Anne, like something which could
not be represented, no longer a human being but simply
a being, marvelously a being, among the mayflies and the
falling suns, with the *agonizing atoms* [*atomes agonisants*],
doomed species, wounded illnesses, ascended the course
of waters where obscure *origins* [*germes*] floundered" (*TO*,

83). The term *germe*[15] appears more than once in *Thomas l'Obscur,* perhaps not exactly in the sense of those syllable-seeds of Indian atomism expressing language's magical value and creative power, but rather as a reminder of that which interested Blanchot in the automatic writing of Breton: the affirmation of "this infinite murmur opened near us, underneath our common utterances, which seems an eternal spring" (*SL,* 181). Hence this, for example: "I made a supreme effort to keep outside myself, as near as possible to the place of *beginnings* [*germes*]. Now, far from achieving as a complete man, as an adolescent, as *protoplasm,* the state of the possible . . ." (*TO,* 97; my emphasis). What Thomas discovers here is the "obscure Thomas," that unnamable clone of nothingness in which his form resides.

Mad Readings

For a few years, between 1906 and 1909, the eminently serious Ferdinand de Saussure, inventor of linguistics, filled a considerable number of notebooks with the anagrams he believed he had found in Saturnine verse.[16] Analyzing this Latin poetry, Saussure set himself to deciphering the combinations of phonemes in which, according to him, one or several verses formed the anagram of a single word (usually a proper noun, such as the name of a god or hero). In what he interpreted as a process of encoding, he believed he had identified a compositional constraint, equal to rhyme in French poetry, or even perhaps a quasi-obsessive ritual . . . but absolutely nothing remotely resembling the élan of inspired writing. This latter point needs to be underlined. There is nothing mystical about this research, Starobinski notes, no notion on Saussure's part of searching for the *vital origin* [*germe vital*] of the poem; at most, he sees his deciphered anagrams functioning as a mnemonic support for the discourse of the improvisational poet, even if he does suggest here and there the idea of an occult tradition and a carefully preserved secret. Very quickly, however, Saussure became worried about the potentially illusory nature of this pursuit of similitude, of diffuse echoes and the concealed repetition of names in Latin verse. The quest, having veered toward obsession, came to a sudden end.

Remember what Barthes said on reading: "the reader's specific site is the paragram, as it obsessed Saussure (did he not feel he was going mad, this scholar, from being solely and completely the reader?): a 'true' reading, a reading which would assume its affirmation, would be a mad reading, not because it would invent improbable meanings (misconstructions), not because it would be 'delirious,' but because it would perceive the simultaneous multiplicity of meanings, of points of view, of structures, a space extended outside the laws which proscribe contradiction."[17] What is a "totally multiple, paragrammatic" reader? Is it the total of virtually possible readings, as structuralism would have it, or is it rather the multiplicity of those voices and acts of attentiveness, scattered and floating, fleetingly held together in a single figure, *this* reader? Hence Thomas, barely a subject, oscillating between nothingness and existence, at times reading, at others writing, infinitely dissociated and plastic, "prodigiously absent" (*TO,* 107).

"As his study of hypograms progressed, Ferdinand de Saussure showed himself capable of finding an increasing quantity of names hidden beneath a line of poetry: four, for instance, within a single line of Johnson's. But if this approach had been further developed, it would soon have become a quagmire. Wave upon wave of possible names would have taken shape beneath his alert and disciplined eye."[18] "Is this the vertigo of error?" Starobinski asks in respect of Saussure, or is it not rather "the discovery of the simple truth that language is an infinite resource, and that behind each phrase lies hidden the multiple clamor from which it has detached itself to appear before us in its isolated individuality"?[19] Saussure searched long and in vain for a method that would allow him to prove that his hypograms were not merely the work of chance. But how could he prove it? How can one end the uncontrollable germination of words opening out into the infinite, end the ever-increasing number of "words beneath words"?[20] He asked himself whether the hypogram or anagram, instead of being the sign of poetic creation itself, might not in fact be a retrospective phantom roused by the reader. Whether it is a verbal latency concealed beneath the words of the poem or a conscious process is a debate that, as Starobinski opportunely reminds us, fascinated theorists of the text during the 1970s: are we dealing here with the author's creative intent or with textual productivity, the work of language? Who, nowadays, would pose the question in such bold terms?

And now I reread the first lines of this chapter and see a sudden proliferation of anagrams and inversions, the dissociation of syllables and phonic echoes, the seeds and atoms of language: "*Il faudra s'interroger un j**our pour** sav**oir** **pour***qu***oi** [One day, we shall have to investigate why][. . .] *une* **ex***périence de l'***extrême** [an experience of the extreme][. . .] *l**oi**sir où chacun ressent par* **pro***je***ction,** *é***pro***uve par identifica**tion,** vit par* **pro***cura**tion** [pastime through which you feel by projection, experience by identification, live vicariously][. . .] *cette* **pro***vis**oi**re 'perte de* **soi**' *dans l'ext**as**e ou le* **sa***cri*fice [the temporary 'loss of self' in ecstasy or sacrifice][. . .]."

"The reader contemplated this little spark of life joyfully, not doubting that he had awakened it," whispered Thomas (*TO*, 25).

BIBLIOGRAPHICAL NOTE

The following articles were published prior to this text and served as a basis for certain chapters. They have been entirely rewritten and elaborated here, or even completely rethought:

"Une audace folle," Europe, no. 901 (May 2004).
"Appartenir, selon Derrida," in *Rue Descartes,* no. 52 (PUF, 2006).
"Le grain de folie d'Emmanuel Levinas," presented at the *Territoires d'Emmanuel Levinas* colloquium, organized by Danielle Cohen-Levinas and Bruno Clément at the *Collège internationale de philosophie* in March 2006.
"Il n'y a pas de métalangage" (Lacan and Beckett), in *Lacan & la littérature,* ed. Éric Marty (Paris: Manucius, 2005).
"Qu'est-ce qu'un archive?" (Beckett, Foucault), in *Présence de Samuel Beckett*, ed. Sjef Houppermans, *Samuel Beckett Today/Aujourd'hui* (Amsterdam and New York: Rodolphi, 2006).
"À la limite," presented at the *Borderless Beckett* colloquium, Waseda University, Tokyo, September 2006.
"Blanchot le Héros" and "Les anagrammes de Blanchot," *Europe,* no. 940–941 (August–September 2007).

NOTES

Translators' Prefatory Note

1. The notable exception here is Sartre, whose analysis of *angoisse* has indeed been rendered in the translation of *Being and Nothingness* by Hazel Barnes as pertaining to "anguish" and not "anxiety." While Grossman's opening chapter refers to Sartre's description of nausea, in his novel of that name, rather than to the analyses of *Being and Nothingness*, "nausea" designates, of course, for Sartre, "existential *angoisse.*"

2. Walter Skeat, *An Etymological Dictionary of the English Language,* 2nd ed. (Oxford: Clarendon Press, 1883).

3. James Strachey, "The Term '*Angst*' and its English Translation," *The Standard Edition of the Complete Psychological Works of Sigmund Freud, Volume III (1893–1899): Early Psycho-Analytic Publications* (London: Hogarth Press, 1962), 116–17.

4. For an elaboration of the philosophical signification acquired by the term *angoisse* in French philosophical texts from the late 1800s on, and the influence of Kierkegaard's book in this respect, see André Lalonde, *Vocabulaire technique et critique de la philosophie* (1926; repr., Paris: Presses Universitaires de France, 1980).

5. Walter Lowrie, "Translator's Preface" to Søren Kierkegaard, *The Concept of Dread* (Princeton, N.J.: Princeton University Press, 1944), xi.

6. Alastair Hannay, "Translator's Note" to Søren Kierkegaard, *The Concept of Anxiety* (London: Norton, 2014), 21.

Out of Oneself

1. Antonin Artaud, "The Umbilicus of Limbo," in *Selected Writings*, ed. Susan Sontag, trans. Helen Weaver (New York: Farrar, Strauss & Giroux, 1976), 71–72.

2. Antonin Artaud, "From Art and Death," in *Selected Writings*, ed. Sontag, 121.

3. "Anguish," from the Old French *anguisse, angoisse*, from Latin *angustia*, "narrowness," which is itself derived from *angustus*, "narrow." The French word *angoisse* retained the sense of a "narrow passage or defile" until the sixteenth century.

4. Martin Heidegger, *What Is Called Thinking?*, trans. J. Glenn Gray (New York: Perennial-HarperCollins, 2004), 231.

5. This, for example, was taken from a "medical" help website: "Overly worried, tired or irritable? You might be suffering from generalized anxiety disorder. This particular form of anxiety is widespread and mostly affects women. What are the symptoms? How do I treat it? Let's take a look at the symptoms and treatments for combatting GAD. Long considered a form of neurosis, generalized anxiety disorder was only recently identified as a separate illness. And yet it's relatively widespread: 4% of the population suffer from it. Woman are twice as likely as men to be affected. Put simply, the disorder affects people who are anxious by nature. GAD occurs as the result of a distressing experience (divorce, losing one's job, etc.), although some people are genetically predisposed. GAD manifests itself as a severe episode of anxiety [*anxiété*] that lasts for a minimum of six months, a period during which the sufferer experiences uncontrollable, chronic worry, for trivial reasons. In addition, there will be at least three of the six following symptoms: fatigue, muscular tension, agitation or overexcitedness, difficulty concentrating, trouble sleeping, and irritability. Other symptoms have also been linked: cold and clammy hands, dry mouth, sweating, nausea or diarrhea, frequent need to urinate (pollakiuria), difficulty swallowing or the sensation of a lump in one's throat, tremors, contractions, pain, aching muscles, irritable bowel syndrome, cephalgia." It would appear that Molière's *Imaginary Invalid* is alive and well on the Internet . . .

6. Georges Bataille, *Inner Experience,* trans. Leslie Anne Boldt (New York: State University of New York Press, 1988), 35.

7. Évelyne Grossman, *La Défiguration* (Paris: Minuit, 2004). In this work, I use the term *"désidentité"* [disidentity] to refer to the invention in modern literature of an escape from oneself that both undoes personal and narcissistic identity (disidentification) and, by the same stroke, elaborates the multiple forms of a shifting identity. [That the multiple identities thus yielded entail the undoing of narcissistic identity can also, in fact, be heard in the French *"des identités"*—"(multiple) identities"—which is a homonym of *"désidentité."*—Trans.]

8. Alain Ehrenberg, *The Weariness of the Self,* trans. David Homel et al., (Montreal: McGill-Queen's University Press, 2010), 44.

9. On the opposition between the concepts of Freud and Janet and the notion of *psychic exhaustion,* see also Marie-Claude Lambotte, *Le Discours Mélancolique* (Paris: Anthropos, 1993), in particular chapter 1, 37–51.

10. Bataille, *Inner Experience,* 33.

11. See Gilles Deleuze, *The Exhausted* (postface to Samuel Beckett's *Quad*), trans. Anthony Uhlmann, in *Substance* 24, no. 3, issue 78 (1995), 3.

12. Emmanuel Levinas, *Existence and Existents,* trans. Alphonso Lingis (London: Kluwer Academic Publishers, 1988), 29–36.

13. Levinas, 24–25, my emphasis.

14. Rather than *anxiety* or *anguish* [*angoisse*], Levinas prefers the terms *fear* and *horror* [*peur, crainte,* and *horreur*]. Rightly or wrongly, anxiety, for him, refers to the phenomenological analysis developed by Heidegger in *Being and Time,* which he understands as a return to the self, a reflective structure of affectivity in which "the *about* and the *for* coincide: anxiety *about* finitude is anxiety *for* my finitude." In this sense, he underlines, "all emotion [for Heidegger], because of this return to the self, goes back to anxiety. It seems to us that the fear for the other does not have this return to the self" (*Ethics and Infinity,* trans. Richard A. Cohen [Pittsburgh: Duquesne University Press, 1985], 119). Although this is not the place to develop such a point, it would be easy to show Levinas's intentional bad faith toward Heidegger's analyses, which he strives to avoid, upturn even,

before sometimes giving them just credit. Hence, in *Otherwise than Being,* his referring to Heidegger's analysis of "anxiety over the limitation of being" (trans. Alphonso Lingis [Dordrecht: Kluwer Academic Publishers, 1991], chapter 4, 194n10). To twist and knowingly "misunderstand" Heidegger, as Levinas explains in an incisive footnote, is also a way not to "deny the debt" owed to him (ibid., 189n28).

15. Jean-Paul Sartre, *Nausea*, trans. Lloyd Alexander (New York: New Directions, 1949), 127.

16. Emmanuel Levinas, *On Escape,* trans. Bettina Bergo, introduced and annotated by Jacques Rolland (Stanford, Calif.: Stanford University Press, 2003), 66–67. My emphasis.

17. Levinas, *Otherwise than Being,* 74.

18. Aristotle, *L'Homme de génie et la mélancholie,* translated into French, introduced and annotated by Jackie Pigeaud (Paris: Rivages poche, "Petite Bibliothèque" collection, 1991), 41. [Our translation from the French.]

19. Bataille, *Inner Experience,* 176.

20. Pierre Janet, *De l'Angoisse à l'extase: Études sur les croyances et les sentiments,* (*Un délire religieux. La croyance*) (Paris: Librairie Félix Alcan, 1926–1928). [No English translation.] An electronic version of Janet's text is available on the Université du Québec à Chicoutimi's website "*Les classiques des sciences sociales*": http://classiques.uqac.ca/classiques/janet_pierre.

21. [Bataille, *Inner Experience,* 119.—Trans.]

22. Michel de Certeau, *Histoire et psychanalyse entre science et fiction* (Paris: Gallimard "Folio-essais", 2002), 219–38.

23. Maurice Blanchot, "Affirmation and the Passion of Negative Thought," in *The Infinite Conversation,* trans. Susan Hanson (Minneapolis: University of Minnesota Press, 2003), 202–11.

24. Michel Foucault, *Maurice Blanchot: The Thought from Outside,* trans. Brian Massumi (New York: Zone Books, 1997), 16.

25. Levinas, *Otherwise than Being,* 93–94.

26. Alexandre Kojève, *Introduction to the Reading of Hegel,* trans. James H. Nichols Jr. (Ithaca, N.Y.: Cornell University Press, 1980), 209–10.

27. Blanchot, "On Nietzsche's Side," in *The Work of Fire* (Stanford, Calif.: Stanford University Press, 1995), 294.

28. Blanchot, *The Infinite Conversation*, 207.

29. Jean-François Lyotard, *The Inhuman*, trans. Geoffrey Bennington and Rachel Bowlby (Stanford, Calif.: Stanford University Press, 1991); *Lessons on the Analytic of the Sublime*, trans. Elizabeth Rottenberg *(*Stanford, Calif.: Stanford University Press, 1994).

30. Pierre Fédida et al., *Humain / Déshumain* (Paris: PUF, 2007), 100–101.

31. See, among others, Melanie Klein, *Contributions to Psychoanalysis (1921–1945)* (London: Hogarth Press, 1950); D. W. Winnicott, *Through Paediatrics to Psychoanalysis* (London: Karnac Books, 1975); Pierre Fédida, *Des Bienfaits de la Dépression* (Paris: Odile Jacob, 2007).

32. Samuel Beckett, *Waiting for Godot* (London: Faber and Faber, 2010), 58.

33. Emmanuel Levinas, *Totality and Infinity*, trans. Alphonso Lingis (Dordrecht: Klewer Academic Press, 1991), 30. My emphasis.

34. Antonin Artaud, "Messages révolutionnaires," in *Œuvres* (Paris: Gallimard, 2004), 728. [Our translation.]

35. Samuel Beckett, *The Unnamable*, ed. Steven Connor (London: Faber and Faber, 2010), 104.

36. Bataille, *Inner Experience*, 84 and 95.

37. Beckett, *Ill Seen Ill Said*, in *Company Ill Seen Ill Said Worstward Ho Stirrings Still*, ed. Dirk Van Hulle (London: Faber and Faber, 2009), 78.

38. [The line reads "*il ne souffle pas le rien*" in Artaud's original. While the verb *souffler* can simply mean "to exhale" or "blow," it can equally be understood, as was often Artaud's intention, in the sense of "to steal" or "spirit away." The reader should be aware that we have had to choose only one of these meanings to render here.—Trans.]

39. Artaud, *Suppôts et Supplications*, in *Œuvres*, 1383. [Our translation.]

40. Jacques Lacan, *Anxiety: The Seminar of Jacques Lacan, Book X*, ed. Jacques-Alain Miller, trans. A. R. Price (Cambridge, UK: Polity Press, 2014), 327. My emphasis.

41. Maurice Blanchot, "Death of the Last Writer," in *The Book to Come*, trans. Charlotte Mandell (Stanford, Calif.: Stanford University Press, 2003), 218–23.

42. Levinas, *Otherwise than Being*, 180–81. My emphasis.

43. Emmanuel Levinas, "On Maurice Blanchot," in *Proper Names,* ed. Werner Hamacher and David E. Wellbery, trans. Michael B. Smith (Stanford, Calif.: Stanford University Press, 1996), 140. [Translation modified.]

44. Levinas, *Totality and Infinity,* in particular 50–51 and 216.

45. Levinas, *Otherwise than Being,* 148–49. My emphasis.

46. [The French word for "verse" or "verses," *"vers,"* is a homonym of *"ver,"* "worm," and it is probable that Artaud is playing on this homonymy in order to reinforce the idea of "stillborn."—Trans.]

47. Artaud, "Revolt against Poetry," in *Artaud Anthology,* ed. Jack Hirschman, trans. Jack Hirschman (San Francisco: City Lights Books, 1965), 100. [Translation modified.]

48. Gilles Deleuze, *Negotiations,* trans. Martin Joughin (New York: Columbia University Press, 1995), 6–7.

49. Louis-René des Forêts, *The Children's Room,* trans. Jean Stewart (London: John Calder, 1963), 192. My emphasis.

50. In *Les Lectures clandestines: emprunts et influences dans l'oeuvre de Louis-René des Forêts* (a doctoral thesis done under the supervision of François Marmande, Paris 7 University, November 2001), Emmanuel Delaplanche gives a very useful list of some of these borrowings, particularly those in *Les Mendiants* (translated as *The Beggars*) and *Le Bavard*. In neither of these works, it seems, are Artaud and Joyce present.

51. On this dread, which was also the dread of Jacques Derrida, see "The Voices of Derrida" in this volume.

52. Blanchot, *The Space of Literature,* trans. Ann Smock (Lincoln: University of Nebraska Press, 1982), 28.

53. Jacques Derrida, *Signéponge/Signsponge,* trans. Richard Rand (New York: Columbia University Press, 1985); "To Unsense the Subjectile," in *The Secret Art of Antonin Artaud,* by Jacques Derrida and Paule Thévenin, trans. Mary Ann Caws (Cambridge, Mass.: MIT Press, 1998).

54. [*"Voler"* translates both as "to fly" and "to steal."—Trans.]

55. [These dates are those of the publication in French of Derrida's texts on Ponge and Artaud.—Trans.]

56. For another sense (resistance to familial and genealogical

identities), see also François Noudelmann, *Hors de moi*, (Paris: Léo Scheer, 2006).

The Voices of Jacques Derrida

1. See, among other places, Jacques Derrida, *Voice and Phenomenon*, trans. Leonard Lawlor (Evanston, Ill.: Northwestern University Press, 2011), 12–13; *Of Grammatology*, trans. Gayatri Chakravorty Spivak (Baltimore: The John Hopkins University Press, 1997), 10–14.

2. Jacques Derrida, "Les Voix d'Artaud (la force, la forme, la forge)," interview with Évelyne Grossman, *Le Magazine Littéraire*, no. 434 (September 2004). [Our translation.]

3. For an analysis of survival/living on [*survivance*] in Nietzsche's work, see Jacques Derrida, "Otobiography," in *The Ear of the Other*, ed. Christie McDonald, trans. Peggy Kamuf (New York: Schocken Books, 1985). [In Derrida's use of the French term "*survivance*" one must hear not only its acceptation of "survival" but also that of "living on."—Trans.]

4. Interview in *Magazine Littéraire*, 35. [Our translation. In French, this quote ends with, ". . . *quelle est ma voie (voix)?*" which plays on the homophony between *voie* (way, approach) and *voix* (voice); this is unfortunately lost in translation.] See also "Artaud, oui . . ." interview with Évelyne Grossman, *Europe* 873–874 (January–February 2002).

5. Geoffrey Bennington and Jacques Derrida, *Jacques Derrida*, trans. Geoffrey Bennington (Chicago: University of Chicago Press, 1993).

6. Jacques Derrida, "Force and Signification," in *Writing and Difference*, trans. Alan Bass (London: Routledge, 2001), 11.

7. Derrida, *Writing and Difference*, 266.

8. Derrida, 22 and 223.

9. One can reread in this light many of Derrida's first texts, which—in *Writing and Difference* and *Dissemination*, for example—revolve around these questions of repetition, double, *mimesis*, imitation, and mimicry of the mime.

10. On all of this, see the text by Derrida referred to here, "Cogito and the History of Madness," in *Writing and Difference*, as well as

the enlightening article by Pierre Macherey, "Mais quoi! Ce sont des fous: retour sur une querelle," available online at www.univ-lille3.fr /set/.

11. Derrida, "Cogito and the History of Madness," 67–68.

12. Jacques Derrida, "Circumfession," in Bennington and Derrida, *Jacques Derrida*, 305–8.

13. See Jacques Derrida, "Chora," trans. Ian McCloud, in *Chora L Works* (New York: Monacelli Press, 1997), and *Rogues,* trans. Pascale Anne Brault and Michael Naas (Stanford, Calif.: Stanford University Press, 2005), among others.

14. Jacques Derrida, *Resistances of Psychoanalysis,* trans. Peggy Kamuf, Pascale-Anne Brault, and Michael Naas (Stanford, Calif.: Stanford University Press, 1998), 30.

15. Blanchot, *The Space of Literature,* 239.

16. Jacques Derrida and Hélène Cixous, "A Silkworm of One's Own," in *Veils,* trans. Geoffrey Bennington (Stanford, Calif.: Stanford University Press, 2002), 36. [As Derrida himself remarks immediately before the passage just cited from *Veils,* "*ça*" is a demonstrative pronoun ("that," "this"), "*sa*" a possessive adjective ("his," "hers," "its"), and "*s'avoir*" ("have each other," "have oneself") a homonym for "*savoir.*"—Trans.]

17. Jacques Derrida, "To Speculate—On 'Freud,'" in *The Postcard*, trans. Alan Bass (Chicago: University of Chicago Press, 1987), 261.

18. Derrida, "Circumfession," 272–73.

19. Jacques Derrida, *Parages,* ed. John P. Leavey, trans. Tom Conley, James Hulbert, John P. Leavey, and Avital Ronnell (Stanford, Calif.: Stanford University Press, 2011), 2.

20. Derrida, "Otobiographies," 6 and 11.

21. Derrida, *Parages,*, 244–49.

22. Bennington and Derrida, *Jacques Derrida,* 327.

23. Jacques Derrida, *Monolingualism of the Other,* trans. Patrick Mensah (Stanford, Calif.: Stanford University Press, 1998), 59–60.

24. Bennington and Derrida, *Jacques Derrida,* 302.

25. Jacques Derrida, *The Other Heading,* trans. Pascale-Anne Brault and Michael B. Naas (Bloomington: Indiana University Press, 1992), 82–83.

26. Régine Robin, "Autobiographie et judéité chez Jacques Derrida," in "Derrida lecteur," eds. Ginette Michaud and Georges Leroux,

special issue, *Études françaises* 38, no. 1–2 (2002), 211. [Our translation.]

27. Derrida, *Monolingualism of the Other,* 14.

28. Derrida, 21.

29. ["Gave place to" is a literal translation of the French "*donna lieu à,*" which would more usually be translated as "gave rise to."—Trans.]

30. [Although both quotes use *appartenir,* "to belong," in the original French—"*Un secret n'appartient pas,*" "*La langue n'appartient pas*"—the second quote was in fact translated as "Language is never owned" in the context of an interview between the author and Jacques Derrida (Jacques Derrida, "Language Is Never Owned," in *Sovereignties in Question,* eds. and trans. Thomas Dutoit and Outi Pasanen, 97–107 (New York: Fordham University Press, 2005).—Trans.]

31. Derrida, *Parages,* 76–78. On this point, also see Michel Lisse, "Comment ne pas dire le dernier mot? ou: Le pas au-delà de la dénégation," in *Logiques et écritures de la negation,* eds. Ginette Michaux and Pierre Piret (Paris: Kimé, 2000), 68–69.

32. Jacques Derrida, *Geneses, Genealogies, Genres, and Genius,* trans. Beverley Bie Brahic (New York: Columbia University Press, 2006), 59–60.

33. Jacques Derrida, *Specters of Marx,* trans. Peggy Kamuf (New York: Routledge Classics, 2006), xvii–xviii.

34. Derrida, xviii

35. Derrida, 221.

36. [The French text uses the expression "Unheimliche *à demeure*" here. It is important to note that "*à demeure*" can mean both "permanently" and "at home," while "*demeure*" alone translates as "domicile" or "dwelling."—Trans.]

37. Derrida, "Otobiographies," 36.

Emmanuel Levinas's Seed of Folly

1. Emmanual Levinas, *Of God Who Comes to Mind,* trans. Bettina Bergo (Stanford, Calif.: Stanford University Press, 1998), 110.

2. Emmanual Levinas, *On Escape*, trans. Bettina Bergo (Stanford, Calif.: Stanford University Press, 2003). On the question of escape as a metaphor for the exit from being in Levinas's work, see

the excellent article by Miguel Abensour entitled "L'extravagante hypothèse," in *Emmanuel Levinas* (Rue Descartes, Collège International de Philosophie, 1998); republished in 2006 by PUF. [No English translation.]

3. Emmanual Levinas, *Otherwise than Being*, henceforth abbreviated to *OB.*

4. Stéphane Mallarmé "Crisis of Verse," in *Divigations,* trans. Barbara Johnson (Cambridge, Mass.: The Belknap Press of Harvard University Press, 2007), 209, 235, 236. [Translation modified.]

5. Jaques Derrida, "At This Very Moment in This Work Here I Am," in *Psyche,* ed. Peggy Kamuf and Elizabeth Rottenberg, trans. Ruben Berezdivin and Peggy Kamuf (Stanford, Calif.: Stanford University Press, 2007).

6. [Translation modified.]

7. Antonin Artaud, fourth letter on language to Jean Paulhan (May 28, 1933), *The Theater and Its Double,* trans. Mary Caroline Richards (New York: Grove Weidenfeld, 1958), 118.

8. [*Figure* translates from French as both as "figure" and as "face"; hence the link between *défiguration* and Levinas' "face" (although the French word Levinas uses in this respect is always "visage").—Trans.]

9. *Totality and Infinity,* p.198.

10. Emmanuel Levinas, "On Maurice Blanchot," in *Proper Names,* trans. Michael B. Smith (Stanford, Calif.: Stanford University Press, 1996), 132–33. [Grossman's emphasis.]

11. Letter to Marthe Robert, 9 May 1946, *Suppôts et Supplicia-tions, Oeuvres* (Paris: Gallimard "Quarto," 2004), 1305. [Our translation.]

12. Levinas, "On Maurice Blanchot," 140.

13. Levinas, 143.

14. Levinas, 151.

15. Levinas,. [Translation modified.]

16. Levinas, 170.

17. Samuel Beckett, *The Unnamable,* ed. Steven Connor (London: Faber and Faber, 2010), 92.

18. Quoted by Jacques Rolland, in Levinas, *On Escape,* 113.

19. Levinas, *God, Death, and Time,* trans. Bettina Bergo (Stanford, Calif.: Stanford University Press, 2000), 131–32.

20. In *Otherwise than Being,* he writes the following on the body and the expression "in one's skin": "The body is not only an image or figure here; it is the distinctive in-oneself of the contraction of ipseity and its breakup" (109).

21. Maurice Blanchot, *Thomas the Obscure,* trans. Robert Lamberton (New York: Station Hill Press, 1988), 25.

22. See further on, page 146 and following.

23. Blanchot, *The Infinite Conversation,* 125.

24. "But *obsession* is not an intentionality once again, as though there were question in it of an aim at some correlative term, however complex it may be. The *obsession* by the other in the face is already the plot of infinity which could not materialize as something correlative and *exceeds* the scope of intentionality. It is the *excession* of the here, as locus, and of the now, as an hour" (*OB,* 193, note 31; my emphasis).

25. See also where he mentions *obsession* a little earlier: "In obsession, the *accusation* effected by categories turns into an *absolute accusative* in which the ego proper to free consciousness is caught up. It is an *accusation* without foundation, to be sure, prior to any movement of the will, an *obsessional* and persecuting *accusation*" (*OB,* 110; my emphasis).

26. "And suddenly I remembered my name, Molloy. My name is Molloy, I cried, all of a sudden, now I remember. [. . .] And your mother? said the sergeant. I didn't follow. Is your mother's name Molloy too? said the sergeant. I thought it over. Your mother, said the sergeant, is your mother's—. Let me think!" (Samuel Beckett, *Molloy,* ed. Shane Weller [London: Faber and Faber, 2009], 20.)

27. On the difference Levinas saw between signifyingness and signification, see, for example, *Otherwise than Being,* 46 and 69.

28. Antonin Artaud, "Lecture at Vieux Colombier, 13 January 1947," *Oeuvres* (Paris: Gallimard, 2004), 1176. [Our translation.]

"There Is No Such Thing as Metalanguage"

1. Jacques Lacan, "Science and Truth," in *Écrits,* trans. Bruce Fink (New York: W. W. Norton & Company, 2006), 736–37.

2. Roland Barthes, "From Science to Literature," in *The Rustle of Language,* trans. Richard Howard (Oxford: Basil Blackwell, 1986), 9–10.

3. Vincent Descombes, *L'Inconscient Malgré Lui* (Paris: Minuit, 1977). [No English translation.]

4. Roland Barthes, "Lecture in Inauguration of the Chair of Literary Semiology, Collège de France, January 7, 1977," trans. Richard Howard, *October* 8 (Spring 1979): 6.

5. Sigmund Freud, "Negation," in *The Standard Edition of the Complete Psychological Works of Sigmund Freud, vol. 19 (1923– 1925),* ed. James Strachey, original trans. Joan Riviere (London: Vintage, 2001), 235; my emphasis.

6. Jacques Lacan, *The Ethics of Psychoanalysis,* trans. Dennis Porter (London: Tavistock/Routledge, 1992), 64.

7. Lacan, 64.

8. Jacques Derrida, "Typewriter Ribbon," in *Without Alibi,* trans. Peggy Kamuf (Stanford, Calif.: Stanford University Press, 2002), 138.

9. [The essay to which this note was added, "Typewriter Ribbon," does not in fact appear in the translation of *Papier Machine* but instead in *Without Alibi.* The note—note 25—can be found on page 296.—Trans.]

10. [The instability of the *ne* referred to by Derrida is only apparent in Lacan's original sentence in French: "La particule négative *ne* vient au jour qu'à partir du moment où je parle vraiment, et non pas au moment où je suis parlé, si je suis au niveau de l'inconscient." Whereas in the translation this "*ne*" features simply as the subject of the sentence, in Lacan's original French it equally functions, surreptitiously as it were, in a restrictive sense—as an element, that is, of the "*ne . . . que*" construction, which translates as "only." Whence the seeming lack of an additional *ne* becomes apparent, as Grossman goes on to discuss.—Trans.]

11. Jacques Lacan, "The Mistaking of the Subject Supposed to Know," trans. Jack W. Stone, from the French version published in *Autres Écrits* (Paris: Seuil, 2001), 329–39. Available: http://web.missouri.edu/~stonej/mistak.pdf.

12. [As Grossman makes clear, "*aucun*" can mean both "any" and "none." Although one is much more likely to read Madame de Sévigné's remark as was intended—"I would be most upset, my dear, were *any* messenger to drown"—the double meaning of the word

gives rise to a potential misunderstanding: "I would be most upset, my dear, were *no* messenger to drown."—Trans.]

13. Lacan, "The Mistaking of the Subject Supposed to Know."

14. *L'Arc,* no. 58 (1974).

15. [It is important to note here that "*maîtrise*" and "*méprise*" are near homophones.—Trans.]

16. Lacan, "The Mistaking of the Subject Supposed to Know"; my emphasis.

17. Beckett, *The Unnamable,* 1.

18. Gilles Deleuze, *Cinema 2: The Time Image,* trans. Hugh Tomlinson and Robert Galeta (Minneapolis: University of Minnesota Press, 1997), 171–72.

19. Beckett, *Molloy,* 52.

20. Lacan, "The Mistaking of the Subject Supposed to Know."

21. Lacan, *Écrits,* 678.

22. This chapter was originally given as a talk at the *Lacan and Literature* symposium (November 2002, Paris 7 University, organized by Éric Marty, Catherine Millot, and Pierre Pachet). Astonishingly—or perhaps not so astonishingly, as the case may be—during the discussion that followed my talk, someone present thought I was criticizing Lacan's discourse when I was in fact doing the exact opposite. Clearly this was a mistaking, a misunderstanding. Playing with denial is not without its risks. In the article I am analyzing here, Lacan writes at the end: "I only expect those I speak to here to confirm the misunderstanding" ("The Mistaking of the Subject Supposed to Know"). Note duly taken.

23. Lacan, "The Mistaking of the Subject Supposed to Know"; my emphasis. [Translation modified.]

24. Lacan, *Écrits,* 341; my emphasis.

25. [The homophony of "*caute*" (a syllable without meaning on its own) and "*coton*" should be noted here, as it is this that Lacan plays on in his acting out of a lapsus consisting in stumbling over the word for "cunning" (*cauteleux* ou *cautèle*).—Trans.]

26. Jacques Derrida, "Le Facteur de la Vérité," in *The Post Card* (Chicago: University of Chicago Press, 1987), 477–79.

27. Lacan, *Écrits,* 339.

What Is an Archive?

1. The first appears in "What Is an Author?" a lecture he delivered to the *Société Française de Philosophie* on February 22, 1969 (Michel Foucault, *Aesthetics, Method, and Epistemology,* ed. James D. Faubion, trans. Robert Hurley et al. [New York: New York Press, 1998], 205).

2. Michel Foucault, "The Order of Discourse," trans. Ian McLeod, in *Untying the Text: A Post-Structuralist Reader,* ed. Robert Young (Boston: Routledge & Kegan Paul, 1981), 51.

3. Foucault's response was published as "*Réponse à une question*" in *Esprit,* no. 371 (1968). [An English translation can be found under the title "Politics and the Study of Discourse," trans. Colin Gordon, in *The Foucault Effect: Studies in Governmentality,* ed. Graham Burchell, Colin Gordon and Peter Miller (Chicago: University of Chicago Press, 1991), 53–72.]

4. Foucault, "Politics and the Study of Discourse," 63.

5. Foucault, 70–72. [In the last sentence of this citation, a typographical error ("their" instead of "there") has been corrected. —Trans.]

6. Samuel Beckett, *Texts for Nothing and Other Shorter Prose, 1950–1976,* ed. Mark Nixon (London: Faber and Faber, 2010), 11.

7. I refer here to Foucault's text *Maurice Blanchot: The Thought from Outside,* trans. Brian Massumi (New York: Zone Books, 1987).

8. Foucault, 13.

9. Foucault, 15.

10. Beckett, "For to End Yet Again," in *Texts for Nothing and Other Shorter Prose,* 151; hereafter cited in the text.

11. Samuel Beckett, "The Expelled," in *The Complete Short Prose, 1929–1989,* ed. S. E. Gontarski (New York: Grove Atlantic, 1995), 49–50; my emphasis.

12. Samuel Beckett, "XIII," in *Texts for Nothing and Other Shorter Prose,* 51.

13. Samuel Beckett, "Stirrings Still," in *The Complete Short Prose,* 260 and 263.

14. Sjef Houppermans, "Chutes sans fin dans *Pour Finir Encore,*" *Samuel Beckett Today / Aujourd'hui,* special issue "Beckett in the 1990s," no. 2 (1993): 219–25.

15. Houppermans, 224. [Our translation.]

16. Samuel Beckett, "Ill Seen Ill Said," in *Nohow On* (London: John Calder, 1989), 59.

17. Beckett, *The Unnamable*, 13; my emphasis.

18. Maurice Blanchot, "Where Now? Who Now?" in *The Book to Come,* trans. Charlotte Mandell (Stanford, Calif.: Stanford University Press, 2003), 210.

19. Blanchot, 211; my emphasis.

20. See Bruno Clément's *L'Oeuvre sans qualité: Rhétorique de Samuel Beckett* (Paris: Seuil, 1994), 282 *et sq.* [No English translation.]

21. Beckett, "The Expelled," 46.

22. Samuel Beckett, "The End," in *The Complete Short Prose,* 81.

23. Samuel Beckett, *Malone Dies* (New York: Grove Press, 1956), 98; my emphasis.

24. Samuel Beckett, "Company," in *Nohow On,* 8; my emphasis.

25. Samuel Beckett, "Lessness," in *Texts for Nothing and Other Shorter Prose,* 129; ,my emphasis.

26. ["*Ciel*" in French means both "sky" and "heaven."—Trans.]

27. Samuel Beckett, *Pour Finir Encore et Autres Foirades* (Paris: Minuit, 1976), 9. [The English version reads as follows, but the grammatical point made by the author is clearer in Beckett's original French: "Thus then the skull makes to glimmer again [. . .]. There in the end all at once or by degrees there dawns and magic lingers a leaden dawn" (151). It is, in short, as though the skull controls its own glimmering, just as the dawn does its own dawning.—Trans.]

28. [It should be noted that phrases such as "it is daytime" and "the day is dawning" are pronominal expressions in French: "*il fait jour*" and "*il se fait jour.*"—Trans.]

29. Jacques Derrida, *Archive Fever,* trans. Eric Prenowitz (Chicago: University of Chicago Press, 1996), 8.

30. Samuel Beckett, "The Lost Ones," in *Texts for Nothing and Other Shorter Prose,* 111–12.

31. Beckett, *Pour Finir Encore et Autres Foirades*, 15. [The translation of this quotation, found on page 153 of *Texts for Nothing and Other Shorter Prose,* reads as follows: "Or murmur from some dreg of life . . ."—Trans.]

32. Beckett, *Pour Finir Encore et Autres Foirades,*13 ["Between him and it bird's-eye view the space grows no less . . ." (152). —Trans.]

33. Beckett, *Pour Finir Encore et Autres Foirades*, 9 ["Remains of the days of the light of day never light so faint as theirs so pale" (151).—Trans.]

At the Limit . . .

1. Samuel Beckett, "That Time," in *The Complete Dramatic Works* (London: Faber and Faber, 2006), 390, 393, and 394. [Further page citations appear in the text.—Trans.]

2. [Note that "keep out the void" was originally written in French as "*contenir le vide,*" which literally means "contain the void." It is from the French, then, that Grossman derives the double meaning discussed here.—Trans.]

3. [Emmanuel Levinas, *Proper Names* (Stanford, Calif.: Stanford University Press, 1996), 136—Trans.]

4. James Knowlson, *Damned to Fame: The Life of Samuel Beckett* (New York: Touchstone, 1997), 532.

5. *Macbeth,* act 5, sc. 5.

6. Beckett, quoted in "Working with Beckett" by Alan Schneider, *On Beckett*, ed. S. E. Gontarski (New York: Anthem Press, 2012), 175–88 at 183.

7. [The English text actually reads "never the same but the same as what," but Grossman's reading is based on the French text in which the final word is "*qui,*" which is to say "who" or "whom" in English.—Trans.]

8. Samuel Beckett, *Proust* (New York: Grove Press, 1957), 4–5.

9. Samuel Beckett, *Watt,* ed. C. J. Ackerley (London: Faber and Faber, 2009), 35.

10. Samuel Beckett, *Malone Dies,* ed. Peter Boxall, (London: Faber and Faber, 2010), 51.

11. Beckett, *Proust,* 8.

12. Beckett, *Proust,* 20.

13. Beckett, *Proust,* 3.

14. Beckett, *Unnamable,* 107.

15. [Gilles Deleuze, "The Exhausted," in *Essays Critical and Clin-*

ical, trans. Daniel Smith and Michael Greco (Minneapolis: University of Minnesota Press, 1997), 154—Trans.]

16. [The French expression used here by Grossman is "*fait jouer.*"—Trans.]

17. David Warrilow, "*La musique, pas le sens,*", *Revue d'Esthétique,* special issue on Samuel Beckett (1990): 253. [Our translation.]

18. Roland Barthes, *The Pleasure of the Text,* trans. Richard Miller (New York: Hill and Wang, 1998), 66. [Translation modified.]

19. Angela Moorjani, *Abysmal Games in the Novels of Samuel Beckett* (Chapel Hill: University of North Carolina Press), 1982.

20. See the chapter 4, entitled "There Is No Such Thing as Metalanguage: Lacan and Beckett."

Blanchot Hero

1. The epigraph in *L'Espace Littéraire,* reprinted by Folio-essais, read "Maurice Blanchot, novelist and critic, *was born in 1907.*" The biographical remark disappeared not long after. The citations given in this chapter from Blanchot's texts come from the following editions: *The Space of Literature,* trans. Ann Smock (Lincoln: University of Nebraska Press, 1989), abbreviated in the text as (*SL*); *Thomas the Obscure,* trans. Robert Lamberton (New York: Station Hill Press, 1988), (*TO*); *The Infinite Conversation,* trans. Susan Hanson (Minneapolis: University of Minnesota Press, 1993), (*IC*); *The Book to Come,* trans. Charlotte Mandell (Stanford, Calif.: Stanford University Press, 2003), (*BC*); *Faux Pas,* trans. Charlotte Mandell (Stanford, Calif.: Stanford University Press, 2001), (*FP*); *The Work of Fire,* ed. Werner Hamacher and David E. Wellbery, trans. Charlotte Mandell (Stanford, Calif.: Stanford University Press, 1995), (*WF*); *The Step Not Beyond,* trans. Lycette Nelson (New York: University of New York Press, 1992), (*SNB*); *Political Writings, 1953–1993,* trans. Zakir Paul (New York: Fordham University Press, 2010), (*PW*).

2. [Led by Charles Maurras, this was a reactionary, ultranationalist movement of the early twentieth century, espousing a politics of strong government and monarchism while rejecting democracy and liberalism as the causes of society's moral decay.—Trans.]

3. Accounts and discussion on this period of Maurice Blanchot's

life are numerous and well known. See, among others: Arthur Cools, *Littérature et engagement (analyse diachronique des critiques littéraires et politiques de Maurice Blanchot, 1931–1943)* (Leuwen: Catholic University of Leuwen, 1994–1995 ; available at www.mauriceblanchot.net); Philippe Mesnard, *Maurice Blanchot, le sujet de l'engagement* (Paris: L'Harmattan, 1996); Leslie Hill, *Blanchot, Extreme Contemporary* (London: Routledge, 1997); Christophe Bident, *Maurice Blanchot, partenaire invisible* (Champ Vallon, 1998).

4. Maurice Blancot, *The Blanchot Reader,* ed. Michael Holland (Oxford: Blackwell, 1995), 213–14.

5. "Nowhere has language ever been so completely given over to its own dereliction as it has been in this book," as Françoise Collin rightly pointed out (*Critique,* no. 229 [June 1966]: 563). [Our translation.]

6. Georges Poulet, "Maurice Blanchot critique et romancier," *Critique* no. 229 [June 1966]: 496 and 492 respectively.

7. Fabrice Pliskin, "Blanchot l'obscur," *Le Nouvel Observateur,* February 24, 2003. [Our translation.]

8. "Death of the Last Writer," (*BC,* 218–23).

9. "The movement of that which slips and steals away: detour itself" ("On forgetting," *IC,* 195).

10. Blanchot says the same about Orpheus the poet in *The Book to Come*: "Having returned to daylight, his role with regard to external authorities is limited to disappearing, soon to be torn to pieces by their delegates, the Maenads, while the daytime Styx, the river of public rumor in which his body was scattered, carries his lyric work, and not only carries it, but wants to make itself the song in it, to maintain in it its own fluid reality, its infinitely murmuring becoming, foreign to any shore" (*BC,* 250).

11. Catherine Malabou, "Derrida's Way: noblesse oblige," *Passions de la littérature, avec Jacques Derrida,* ed. Michel Lisse (Paris: Galilée, 1996).

12. "Dying, writing, do not take place, there where someone generally dies, where someone generally writes" (*SNB,* 89).

13. Fédida et al., *Humain / Déshumain,* 11–12.

14. "That ideal reader suffering from an ideal insomnia," *Finnegans Wake* (London: Faber and Faber, 1939), 120.

15. Fédida, *Humain / Déshumain,* 116. [Our translation.]

Blanchot's Anagrams

1. Marcel Proust, *In Search of Lost Time, Volume 1: Swann's Way*, trans. C. K. Scott Moncrieff and Terence Kilmartin (London: Vintage, 1996), 99.

2. Bataille, *Inner Experience*, 116.

3. "I say: a flower! And [. . .] arises musically the fragrant idea itself, the absent flower of all bouquets," Stephane Mallarmé, *Variations sur un sujet* (1895), *Oeuvres Complètes*, ed. H. Mondor et G. Jean-Aubry (Paris: Gallimard, "Bibliothèque de la Pléiade" collection, 1945), 368. The translation of this line appears in the Introduction to *Collected Poems and Other Verse*, trans. E. H. and A. M. Blackmore (Oxford: Oxford University Press, 2006), xvii.

4. [Here, Grossman is alluding to the opposition Derrida saw in Plato's work between the supposed living voice of speech and the dead letter of writing. One might also see in the expression "*lettre morte*" (of which "dead letter" is a direct equivalent in English) the evocation of Hegel's "dead" writing or the homonym "*l'être morte* [dead being]."—Trans.]

5. Jacques Rancière, *Mute Speech*, trans. James Swenson (New York: Columbia University Press, 2011), 35–36.

6. Cf. Serge Viderman, *La Construction de l'Espace Analytique* (Paris: Gallimard, 1982). [No English translation.]

7. Consider: "incapable of seizing again the sense of these metamorphoses and the goal of this silent walk" (*TO*, 61); "Death was a crude metamorphosis beside the indiscernible nullity which I nevertheless coupled with the name Thomas" (*TO*, 91); "[. . .] by means of a metamorphosis which saves me for myself" (*TO*, 99); "Fright, terror, the metamorphosis passes all thought" (*TO*, 103); "A stone rolled, and it slipped through an infinity of metamorphoses the unity of which was that of the world in its splendor" (*TO*, 114).

8. A few examples: "betrayed fatality," abandon, Racinian passion (*TO*, 69); "this so tepid and facile nothingness which Pascal, though already terrified, inhabited" (*TO*, 62–63); Kant's "pure reason" and "critical moment" (*TO*, 63); the Dantesque circles of Hell (*TO*, 63); Artaud's "nothingness with neither sex nor sexual parts" (*TO*, 67).

9. Franz Kafka, *The Metamorphosis and Other Stories*, trans. Stanley Appelbaum (New York: Dover Publications, 1996), 41.

Blanchot read and always cited Alexandre Vialatte's translation (*La Métamorphose,* Gallimard, "Folio" collection, 1955—Vialatte's neg-ligent translation, as he called it), originally published in *N.R.F.* in 1928. Speaking of Gregor, that antihero of the human condition, Blanchot writes, "he still struggles for his place under the sofa, for his little excursions on the coolness of the walls, for life amid the filth and dust" ("Reading Kafka," in *WF,* 10).

10. *Thomas l'Obscure* (Paris: Gallimard, 1941), 23. My emphasis. [Our translation. It would seem that there exists no English transla-tion of the original 1941 version.—Trans.] Of course, the first ver-sion of this text bore the subtitle "novel," which disappeared in the second version, published in 1950.

11. Emmanuel Levinas, *On Escape,* trans. Bettina Bergo (Stan-ford, Calif.: Stanford University Press, 2003), 54. Levinas and Blan-chot, having met at the University of Strasbourg around 1925, re-mained close friends until Levinas's death in 1995. [The translation has been modified to correct a typographical error: "a exit" has been amended to "an exit."—Trans.]

12. Bident, *Maurice Blanchot, partenaire invisible,* 141. [Our translation.] Let us remind ourselves of one or two definitions: an anagram is a word formed by the transposition of letters from an-other word (e.g. *gear* and *rage*). A cryptogram adds a layer of secre-cy. Saussure's hypogram, as we will soon see, refers to an encoded name, the syllables of which are repeated throughout a poem.

13. [The punctuation in this quotation from the English transla-tion of Blanchot's book has been slightly modified.—Trans.]

14. [The phonemes that constitute "(*cet*) *être*" (printed in bold) are scattered throughout the quoted text, as though the word is sur-reptitiously propagating itself therein: their occurrence out of se-quence constantly alludes to but does not explicitly form the word. It is the homonymy of the highlighted phonemes, syllables, and words that allows the anagram to function here, e.g., between "*cet êtr/*" and "*/ssait . . . terr/.*"—Trans.]

15. [The term is translated as "seed," "origin," and "beginning," depending on context. In French, "*germe*" can equally mean germ or bacteria, hence the link to protoplasm.—Trans.].

16. These manuscripts were published and annotated by Jean

Starobinski in *Words upon Words,* trans. Olivia Emmet (New Haven. Conn.: Yale University Press, 1979).

17. Barthes, "On Reading," in *The Rustle of Language,* 42.

18. Starobinski, *Words upon Words,* 122.

19. Starobinski, 122.

20. [In order to correctly render the meaning, the literal translation of Starobinski's French title has been used here instead of the title of the English-language publication, *Words upon Words*—Trans.]

Évelyne Grossman has written on modernist thinkers, including the books *La défiguration: Artaud, Beckett, Michaux* and *Artaud, L'aliéné authentique*. She is a professor at University of Paris VII.

Louise Burchill teaches, translates, and publishes in the fields of contemporary French philosophy, aesthetics, and feminist thought. Her translations include three books by Alain Badiou and numerous texts by Julia Kristeva.

Matthew Cripsey studied philosophy and French. He has a degree in translation studies.